GERONIMO

GERONIMo

Fine Dining in Santa Fe

Cliff Skoglund, Eric DiStefano, and Chris Harvey

with Judyth Hill

TEN SPEED PRESS

Berkeley | Toronto

Ten Speed Press
P.O. Box 7123
Berkeley, California 94707
www.tenspeed.com

Distributed in Australia by Simon & Schuster Australia, in Canada by Ten Speed Press Canada, in New Zealand by Southern Publishers Group, in South Africa by Real Books, and in the United Kingdom and Europe by Airlift Book Company.

Cover design by Jeff Puda
Book design by Betsy Stromberg
Photography by Peter Vitale (except as noted below)
Photograph (left) on page xvi Courtesy Museum of New Mexico, neg. no. 137029
Photograph (right) on page xvi by Janine Guercio, Courtesy Museum of New Mexico, neg. no. 30414
Photograph on page xvii by Karl Kernberger, Courtesy Museum of New Mexico, neg. no. 51224

Library of Congress Cataloging-in-Publication Data

Geronimo: fine dining in Santa Fe / Cliff Skoglund . . . [et al.].
    p. cm.
 ISBN 1-58008-491-5
    1. Cookery. 2. Geronimo (Restaurant) I. Skoglund, Cliff. II. Geronimo (Restaurant)

TX714.G49 2004
641.5--dc22

                                                2004046003

Printed in China
First printing, 2004

1 2 3 4 5 6 7 8 9 10 — 10 09 08 07 06 05 04

Contents

First Courses

Seared Foie Gras with Fresh Berries, Caramelized Maui Pineapple, Amish Apple Butter, and Port Wine Reduction, 35

Pan-Braised Veal Sweetbreads with Savory Green Apple Polenta, 37

Foie Gras Tortellini with Glace de Viande and Green Peppercorns, 40

Mesquite-Grilled Foie Gras Terrine with Sweet Grapes and Verjus, 43

Escargots with Tomato Caper Vinaigrette, 44

Warm Maine Lobster Terrine with Baby Greens and Mustard Sauce, 46

Grilled Lobster Tails with Homemade Angel Hair Pasta and Spicy Chili Mayonnaise, 50

Maryland Blue Crab Cakes with Caviar Sauce and Braised Leeks, 53

Scallop Mousse with Basil Lemon Espuma, 55

Ahi Tuna, Smoked Salmon, and Avocado Tartare with Snap Pea and Gari Salad and Chive Buttermilk Pancakes, 57

Crispy Skate on Rocket Salad with Lime and Shrimp Vinaigrette, 61

Morel Mushroom Tarts with Foie Gras and Black Truffle, 63

Egg Griddled Goat Cheese and Smoked Salmon with Chicory Salad and Crispy Lardons, 66

Entrées

Mesquite-Grilled Peppery Elk Tenderloin with Garlic Confit Potatoes and Exotic Mushroom Sauce, 71

Grilled Veal Porterhouse Steaks with Sweet Potato Flan and Prosciutto Caper Sauce, 74

Tournedos of Beef with Spinach Potato Flan, Port Reduction Sauce, and Herb Garlic Compound Butter, 79

Wasabi-Crusted Rack of Colorado Lamb with Ginger Mint Syrup and Fried Soba Noodle Cakes, 81

Mushroom and Marrow Crusted Strip Steak with Green Peppercorn Sauce and Fondant Potatoes, 84

Stuffed Roasted Loin of Lamb with Leek Fondue and Yukon Gold Potato Quiche, 88

"Quick" Braised Rabbit Saddle with Matzo Scallion Dumplings and Fresh Soybeans, 91

Grilled Rack of Lamb with a Creamy Compote of Fingerling Potatoes, Bacon, and Sweet Corn, 94

Salads

Baby Arugula Salad with Black Truffle Croque Monsieurs, 142

Heirloom Tomatoes with Spanish Blue Cheese and Walnut "Pâté" with Fresh Herb Salad, 145

Mizuna Salad with Maple-Glazed Smithfield Ham and Creamy Buttermilk Hazelnut Vinaigrette, 147

Baby Butter Lettuce with a Warm Heirloom Tomato and Goat Cheese Tart and Garlic Confit Vinaigrette, 148

Italian Prosciutto Wrapped Baby Greens with Black Truffle Vinaigrette, 150

Spring Dandelion Salad with Warm Crispy Shallots, Shaved Tuscan Pecorino, Quail Eggs, and Sweet Lemon and Tuscan Olive Oil Vinaigrette, 153

Summer Cherry Salad with Honey Vinaigrette, 154

Desserts

Pizzelle, 159

Griddled "Elephant Heart" Plum Hotcakes with Rich Tahitian Vanilla Ice Cream, 160

Chocolate Tart, 162

Poire-Williams Soup with Warm Bosc Pears, Star Anise Ice Cream, and Black Pepper Génoise, 163

Star Anise Ice Cream, 166

Meyer Lemon Semifreddo with Basil Seed Sauce, 167

El Ray Venezuelan Milk Chocolate Mousse Pies with Macadamia Nut Crust and Caramelized Bananas, 170

Pistachio Ice Cream, 172

Toasted Coconut Shortbread with Cinnamon Ice Cream and Caramel Apple Sabayon, 173

Eggnog Crème Brûlée with Burgundy Poached Seckel Pears, 175

Chocolate and Cinnamon Pound Cake Pudding, 178

Flourless Chocolate Cakes with White Chocolate Vanilla Sauce, 181

Velarde Apple Normandy, 182

White Peach Shortcake with Warm Buttermilk Biscuits and Honey Crema, 183

Tequila Lime Tarts, 186

Eric's . . . Acknowledgments

*F*or me, this book is about gratitude, and about appreciation for the people who have helped me and patiently guided me.

First and foremost, I want to thank my friend Cliff Skoglund for letting me be a part of his dream, and for letting us all enjoy the view as we sit on the wings of his flight.

Gratitude to Chef Mark Miller, for inspiring all the up-and-coming chefs in our town to do their best, and to keep making that best even better.

Enormous thanks and indebtedness to Heinz Hautle, who is, to me, the greatest chef in the world, for the skills and dedication to excellence that he passed on to all of his apprentices. When I think of what it truly means to be a chef and teacher, in every aspect, Heinz Hautle is without equal. Toques off to you, Chef!

Many thanks to George Mahaffey for his generosity, his support of my career, and his ability to create magnificent cuisine in every kitchen he has ever graced.

And to pastry chef extraordinaire Russell Dingeldein, who raised the standards for the fine art of baking in a small Pennsylvania chocolate town, for his example of unflagging commitment to precision and perfection.

To my buddy Rory Reno, a tremendous chef and culinarian, thank you for teaching me to appreciate the importance of taste, and that a properly cooked bowl of "hunting camp" pot roast can be divine.

Thanks to Daniel Boulud for his faith in me, which led to my opportunity to run my first kitchen in Santa Fe. And for inviting me to work, for that short time, in his most amazing kitchen!

To our exceptionally talented photographer, Peter Vitale, who made those months of shooting the pictures for this book a total pleasure.

Much credit and thanks to my dedicated and gifted right-hand men, executive sous chef Charles Thompson, and chef de cuisine Jose Rodriguez for the extra hours, input, and time they spent testing recipes and keeping the kitchen running as smoothly as ever while this cookbook was being written.

Dearest Jeanne, thank you for your contagious creative talent. And for standing by me all the time and especially through all the hours of writing, and re-writing the cookbook.

Thank you, Judyth (Judy), for teaching me to love words and for being so talented, knowledgeable, poetic, and patient. I can't imagine taking on this monumental task with anyone else.

I would also be amiss if I did not thank Carrie Rodrigues and Betsy Stromberg for the awesome job they did editing and designing this book. Also, to Phil Wood and Dennis Hayes for making Ten Speed Press just the best.

And to Mom and Dad, you have been so supportive, for so long. Thanks for your words of encouragement, and for the example Dad has always set for me of his strong work ethic, which has become my own. But most of all, thanks for teaching me the joy of giving, and finding, happiness in cooking for friends.

And to Sara, for it all!

Cliff's . . . Acknowledgments

*M*uch gratitude and thank you—

To my friend, Chef DiStefano: My professional and personal affiliation with Eric was the inspiration for this book. I felt it utterly essential for connoisseurs of great cuisine to experience his work, regardless of whether or not they had the opportunity to dine at Geronimo. I've always espoused my belief that Eric is a better man than he is a chef. Anyone familiar with the radiance of his food—the readers of this book included—will understand the gravity of that statement.

To my right hand man, Chris Harvey: From humble beginnings as a waiter and a quick ascension to GM, his dedication and devotion to all that we do and the fact that he reminded me of myself when I was his age made it very easy and deserving to offer him a partnership. His continued and steadfast commitment has been a solid buttress to Geronimo and myself.

To John Silver: The best country lawyer and friend a guy could ask for.

To "Lovely" Lois Brennad: Thankfully, she's learned to take it all like water off a duck's back . . . She's my indispensable right hand girl.

To Peter Vitale: Intuitive, patient, and like myself, continually demanding that his work always be the utmost quality. He is perpetually focused on superiority in his efforts.

To Judyth Hill: A staunch Geronimo supporter from day one, she is creative, brilliant, and delightfully wacky. I can think of none other with the capacity, knowledge, and foresight to have helped in the writing of this book.

To the Geronimo staff: They have always been willing and able to rise to the next level of my ever-increasing expectations. The constant effort to hone and perfect the Geronimo experience is greatly appreciated.

To Dennis Hayes at Ten Speed Press: His belief in and support of this project allowed us to create the book we envisioned.

To our loyal customers: I hope you will enjoy this book as much as we enjoyed its preparation!

And finally, to Robert: In the restaurant business, it is often said that you must be married to your restaurant. It takes an incredibly unique and wonderful person to understand that all-encompassing love affair and share that passion—he's my rock and I'm lucky and grateful.

Geronimo History: The Land and the Building

*O*ur story begins, as so many Santa Fe stories do, with the sale of a piece of land in what was then known as La Villa Real de la Santa Fé de San Francisco de Assisi. A town dedicated to St. Francis and Holy Faith.

The Geronimo story remains an ongoing chronicle of faith, faith in the possibility of creating and sustaining an enduring dream.

The year is 1753, and the land is a tract of about 35 acres of farmland in what is now the Canyon Road area.

According to the deed of sale, a soldier of the royal garrison, Isidro Martín, sold to Gerónimo Lopez "for now and forever," a parcel of land for the sum of 52 pesos whose boundaries were "on the east, an arroyo leading to the acequia madre; on the north, the public road leading to the Sierra, on the west the lands of the grantor, Ysidro Martín, and on the south, the acequia madre."

On this piece of land, "in the year of our Lord, 1756," Gerónimo built an adobe house for himself, his wife, Maria Gertrudes Montaño, and their 12 children. They raised ewes, breeding rams, and goats. They had a few burros, 3 bull oxen, and an ox. They grew a fruit orchard of 14 trees. All of these he passed along to his wife and children at the time of his death in 1769, along with household furniture and "outdoor implements, consisting of 2 axes, 2 hoes, 1 copper pot, a spit, spoon and griddle."

Maria later divided up ownership of the rooms in their house and had a separate deed written up for each, leaving each child a room.

Sometime after 1769, the house was purchased by Gerónimo Gonzalez.

In 1839, the Borregos, a leading family in the social and political life of New Mexico, bought all of the extant deeds to the various rooms and reunited the house as a single piece of property. They added the large front room, or *sala,* facing the street, and it served as the scene for many colorful and joyous gatherings, as it does to this day.

In the latter part of the nineteenth century, the brick copings and painted millwork were added, giving the building its current Territorial look.

The family sold the property in 1900, and the house was used for both residences and various retail businesses.

The house was lovingly and painstakingly restored in 1928 by its owner, Mrs. Charles H. Dietrich, and won the Cyrus McCormick prize for best restoration of a residence during the preceding two years.

By 1969, the Borrego House had been added to the Santa Fe registry of historic buildings, honoring both its longevity and its exemplary combination of classic adobe style with early Territorial architecture.

Cliff Skoglund, pursuing his dream, purchased the building in 1990 and opened Geronimo, serendipitously named after the original owners, adding an illustrious chapter of culinary history to the Geronimo legend.

Eric and Judyth on . . . How to Use the Cookbook

*I*t was a tremendous pleasure to write this cookbook for you, our readers and, we hope, frequent dining guests.

We know that some of the techniques we describe may, at first glance, seem a bit daunting.

We can promise you, though, that with a little patience, you too can have wonderful results with our recipes.

The first step, and the best advice we can give, is to read the recipe all the way through, and check to see if you have the equipment, the ingredients, and the advance time.

Whatever you are missing, you can gather, or borrow, or substitute, when that's reasonable. Decide what can or must be made ahead, and plan your prep time accordingly, so that the cooking and serving is, in itself, fun!

As you work your way through the ingredient lists, you will discover that we have occasionally referred to hard-to-find items or to an especially fine ingredient or a favorite source that we want to share with you. You will find a list of these sources and resources on page 220.

When shopping for the ingredients to a recipe, take along a clear and careful list, noting down the amounts called for, and consider purchasing a bit more than you need, just in case.

On page 223, there is a glossary of unusual ingredients and cooking terms. We've tried to make your experience of navigating the recipes both enriching and fun, and we hope that you will find answers to at least some of your questions in that section.

If any of the techniques seem complicated, read them through a few times, and trust yourself! We have worked hard to make sure that our recipes are truly doable, and that the dish you yourself prepare will be as much of a delight in your dining room as in ours.

In many of the recipes, we list salt and pepper without calling for specific amounts. Start by adding a pinch or so, and continue adding the seasonings in small increments until you know what "to your taste" means for you.

We occasionally mention the use of certain equipment, like a Griswold, rondeau, or chinois; these are the utensils we use in our kitchen, but they are not absolute musts. Use what you have, what works for you, and you will have good results. We just wanted to offer you the option to learn what we use!

And sometimes, I just have a fondness for a certain kind of equipment, such as, for stirring heavy items like risotto or polenta, I often mention using a wooden spoon. That's because, when I was growing up, my Mom always used wooden spoons. And for good reason! They don't scrape metal on metal in pots, they feel great to use, they're sturdy, and they absorb heat, so you won't burn your mouth, when you taste Mom's simmering Bolognese!

Another way to add to your enjoyment and success in using this book is to read the introductions to the recipes. Many of them describe the creative impulses behind the recipe—the flavors, textures, and aromas that evolved into a specific dish. These introductions will, we hope, inspire you to develop your own recipes and use components of this book to create signature dishes. For example, the polenta recipe is foolproof and is delicious with a whole array of other items, say, to accompany your favorite roasted chicken recipe, or for a nice, simple lunch, serve a mound of it with a salad of your local greens: heavenly! Be guided by your own hankering and creativity: add some grilled shrimp to the mizuna salad, or serve the black truffle Croque

Monsieurs alone as a passed hors d'oeuvre for a dinner party.

A trick to remember in using this cookbook is that the index has been carefully prepared to include all the subrecipes—salads, vegetables, pastas, potato or rice dishes—that are included as parts of whole dishes but that can also stand on their own. In a cookbook organized differently, these might even have been featured in a separate chapter. We wanted to share with you the recipes for entire meals as they are prepared and served at Geronimo.

If you are planning a dinner party and want to try a special potato or ravioli or risotto recipe, or use our recipe for crêpes, look up these side dishes in the index and combine them with your own menu.

In our opinion, there is a secret gift in this cookbook. That is the chapter entitled "Little Critical Recipes." This is a collection of tried-and-true recipes for the basic and often most important parts of our cuisine. There are recipes for a range of fundamental items—aïoli, vinaigrettes, a variety of stocks—that, once mastered, you will make over and over.

We finish nearly all of the recipes with plating instructions. These are certainly optional. It's just that so frequently our guests at the restaurant are intrigued by the arrangement of the food on their plates as they arrive at table. We are often complimented on the beauty and interesting asymmetry of our presentations, and it is true: we work hard on the visual elements of the dishes. Just by becoming aware of the possibilities and following some of the principles underlying our arrangements, you too will soon be making a grilled piece of meat on a bed of mashed potatoes with mushroom sauce look like it's ready to be on the cover of a gourmet magazine.

Then there is the pure pleasure of perusal. Should this become a favorite picture book that sits on your coffee table for guests to oooh and ahhh over, we won't be offended.

Finally, this is really a story—about good food and good times, it's about Cliff, it's about me, and it's about Geronimo, so that you can be backstage with us as we produce the Geronimo experience.

Everything at Geronimo is tasted in the process of preparation and finish, a lesson I learned very young when I began working at the Hotel Hershey as a saucier's apprentice.

Eric on . . . Pocket of Spoons

Preparing one of the first soups that I had the privilege to make, Champagne and Scallop Soup, which you will find among these pages, I thought I had done well, because I had followed the recipe precisely. As I walked out the door to leave at shift's end, the chef saucier ran after me waving a spoon, shouting in his thick French accent, "Did you taste your soup? Did you taste your soup?"

Obviously, he had!

I went back; he made me taste the soup. Yes, it was a bit flat. Humbled, head hung low, I fixed it. Since that moment I have tasted everything I have ever cooked.

It is one of the most important principles a serious cook can learn. I work to instill it in the young chefs that come to cook at Geronimo. In the kitchen, wielding spoon after spoon, we taste, taste, taste throughout the processes of cooking and the finish of seasoning. Knowing when to use fresh herbs versus dried; choosing between black, red, white, green, or pink pepper; selecting a particular flavor of vinegar—these, among many other subtle discriminations, are critical.

This kind of knowing is trained by tasting: the way a fine sommelier recognizes and understands his wines, so too, should a fine cook develop a savvy palate, the ability to refine and adjust a dish according to his trained sensibilities.

A chef needs to be keenly alert, skilled, and present in all his or her senses. A chef must know what a ripe peach tastes like, know the flavor, feel, and look of a well-marbled piece of meat, the aroma of correctly caramelized onion, and, most critical yet deceptively simple, how to use salt.

Salt is an important, if not the most important, spice: too much and a dish is ruined; too little and it falls flat.

Salt must be added at the right time.

A good example is the salting of meat: since salt draws out moisture from almost anything it touches, if meats are seasoned too soon before cooking, valuable juices are pulled out, and the meat becomes dry. When seasoning a steak, it's occasionally important to kind of melt salt into the flesh; however, most of the time it is best to rub the meat with salt and pepper immediately before searing or grilling it, followed by a few sprinkles of an excellent salt, fleur de sel or gray sea salt, to finish before serving. This seasons the meat to its full flavor potential. It is also imperative to add salt to boiling water before blanching green vegetables, or they lose color and vitality.

The importance of these understandings is immeasurable, and they cannot be learned from a book, though the philosophies can be imparted. It's the day in and day out of the kitchen, observing, imitating, perfecting. It's questioning other chefs and always being driven by one's own desire. That's where the love of it all sinks into the heart and the educated senses of a chef are developed.

Many young professionals interview to train in the Geronimo kitchen. Because of our reputation, they know they will be using the finest ingredients available and receiving extensive and intensive instruction.

As in any demanding profession, only the strong survive. The ones who persevere, who work to excel, are respected and well rewarded.

During my five-year European-style apprenticeship, I learned a great deal from chefs that had that drive seasoned with maturity and wisdom.

I remember finishing my pantry shift in the kitchen and asking the chef Saucier, one of my most important mentors, George Mahaffey, "Chef, can I help you?"

Standing on the line and working with him was a tremendous honor. He was a profoundly generous teacher, constantly offering gleaming insights, hard-won gems of culinary wisdom: To pull a simmering sauce or stock to one side of the flame so the impurities gather on the other side, making it easy to skim with a ladle and thus clarifying the sauce; to thoroughly dry the skin of a meat or fish and thus attain perfect crusting when searing.

George was a consummate professional and perfectionist. He taught me never to accept an inferior *mise en place.* I remember well, after those 12-hour days, George would say, "Hey, I need 3 quarts, equal parts, carrot, celery, and onion brunoise for osso buco tomorrow." That's 3 quarts of perfectly tiny-diced vegetables. And they better be perfect!

After another two hours cutting and watching him during dinner service, I would scrub down his line, cover and date the prep for the next day, still with the attitude—Done chef, got another task...

After that he might talk about food and taste, sometimes sharing a glass of Bordeaux. How fortunate I was, a nervous young apprentice, listening to a great chef sharing his love of food and the business.

And this, along with many other moments, hours, days, years in kitchens I have worked in, has been a 20-year education. Those stories continue. Always beginning with the simple lesson of grabbing a spoon and tasting: that make it or break it moment: subtle and yet, all-important.

Amuses-Gueules

Martini Shots

We first served this particular amuse at a cocktail party at the governor's mansion. The servers walked around with big silver trays lined with shallow mini-martini glasses filled with a little half-melted Grey Goose vodka sorbet, cucumber purée, sweet onions, and crème fraîche, topped with a big dollop of osetra caviar. The guests were abuzz as to whether to eat or drink this little hors d'oeuvre. Very soon the idea caught on and everyone was shooting them back as a cowboy would a shot of rye at the bar, swishing this blast of a sweet, sour, creamy, and salty concoction around in their mouths. Needless to say, they are a lot of fun. The only day-ahead preparation is the vodka sorbet and the crème fraîche.

VODKA SORBET

1 cup premium vodka

1/2 cup peeled, seeded, and puréed cucumber

1 cup simple syrup (page 211)

1 cup spring water

1 teaspoon freshly squeezed lemon juice

1 cup, peeled, seeded, and finely shredded cucumber

1 tablespoon very finely diced sweet onion

1 cup crème fraîche (page 206)

2 ounces osetra or other caviar

8 small sprigs baby dill, for garnish

To prepare the sorbet, combine the vodka, cucumber purée, simple syrup, water, and lemon juice in a bowl and mix well.

Freeze in an ice cream maker, according to the manufacturer's instructions. Place in an airtight container, cover, and store in the freezer until ready to serve. Because of the high alcohol content of the sorbet, it will be a little slushy—perfect for this recipe.

To assemble the shots, place 8 shallow martini glasses on a tray. Spoon a small mound of the shredded cucumber into each glass, and top with a small portion of the sweet onion. With a teaspoon or small ice cream scoop, scoop out 8 nicely rounded servings of the vodka sorbet, and place one in each glass. Don't worry if it melts a bit while you are preparing the rest. Place a dollop of the crème fraîche on the sorbet, and top that with a generous dollop of caviar.

Place a sprig of dill on each, and serve immediately.

Sautéed Quail Breast with White Corn Polenta Cake and Balsamic Syrup

Serves 6

Coming up with new tasters is a lot of fun, and this miniature dish is a wonderful example. We take a boneless quail breast, soak it in an Asian-style marinade, sauté it quickly, and place it on a soft little polenta cake. We then drizzle a bit of balsamic syrup over the top and finish with some spicy baby greens.

The cornmeal we use for these cakes is made from an heirloom variety of white corn, grown by traditional Iroquois farmers in western New York State. They roast the kernels before grinding them into meal, which gives the flour an especially rich, toasty flavor. For a source of this cornmeal, see page 221.

The polenta part of this recipe is more than you will need to make these amuses, but it can be saved, wrapped tightly, in the refrigerator for up to one day. It's delicious fried for breakfast, with eggs and pico de gallo.

MARINADE

2 tablespoons soy sauce

1 tablespoon oyster sauce

1 teaspoon toasted sesame oil

1 tablespoon minced green onion

1/2 teaspoon honey

Freshly squeezed juice of 1 lemon

3 whole quail breasts, boned, skin on

POLENTA

2 tablespoons unsalted butter

1/2 teaspoon minced shallot

1/2 teaspoon minced garlic

3 cups half-and-half

11/2 cups blonde chicken stock (page 213)

1 sprig thyme

1/4 teaspoon freshly ground white pepper

1 cup white cornmeal

3/4 cup grated Romano cheese

Olive oil, for sautéing

1 cup mixed spicy baby greens, such as mustard, arugula, and tatsoi

Freshly squeezed juice of 1/2 lemon

1 tablespoon extra virgin olive oil

Pinch of salt

2 grinds of black pepper

1 tablespoon balsamic reduction (page 203)

To prepare the marinade, combine the soy sauce, oyster sauce, sesame oil, green onion, honey, and lemon juice in a bowl, and whisk well.

Cut the quail breasts in half, leaving a small bit of the skin, and discard the excess skin. Place the quail in a shallow, nonreactive baking dish. Pour the marinade over the quail breasts and cover with plastic wrap. Set in the refrigerator for at least 1 hour, or up to 12 hours.

Generously butter a 12 by 12 by 3/4-inch-deep baking pan.

To prepare the polenta, in a heavy-bottomed saucepan, melt the butter over medium-low heat until slightly bubbly. Add the shallot and garlic and cook for about 1 minute, until the shallot is translucent, taking care not to brown the butter. Add the

half-and-half, stock, thyme, and white pepper, and increase the heat to medium. Simmer for 3 minutes, at a low boil, and then remove the thyme sprig.

Whisking constantly, slowly pour the cornmeal into the simmering cream. Decrease the heat and continue to cook, stirring constantly with a wooden spoon, for about 5 minutes, until the polenta thickens and pulls away from the sides of the pan. Remove from the heat, and fold in the cheese. While the polenta is still warm, pour it into the prepared baking pan. With a spatula lightly rubbed with oil to prevent it from sticking, smooth the surface until it is flat and even. Let cool for 15 minutes, then cover tightly with plastic wrap and set in the refrigerator for about 1 hour, until it is firm to the touch.

Remove the polenta from the refrigerator. With a 2-inch round cookie cutter, cut 6 circles out of the polenta, and set aside. Reserve the remainder of the polenta for another use.

Remove the quail breasts from the marinade, and pat dry with a paper towel.

Heat a small sauté pan over medium-high heat and coat the bottom with a thin layer of olive oil. Sauté the polenta cakes in small batches, turning once, for about 1 minute per side, until golden brown. Set on paper towels to drain.

In the same pan, sauté a quail breast, skin side down, for about 2 minutes, just until nicely browned. Turn over and sauté the other side for 2 minutes, until browned. Repeat with the remaining quail, taking care not to burn them: the marinade has a high sugar content and it will burn easily if not watched carefully. Set aside in a warm place.

To prepare the finishing salad, toss the baby greens in a small bowl with the lemon juice, oil, salt and pepper.

Place a polenta circle on each of 6 small plates. Top each with a quail breast, and delicately drizzle a little of the balsamic reduction over the quail and plate. Set a bit of the salad on each quail breast and serve.

Green Curry Shrimp with Rice Vinegar Cucumbers

Serves 4

We use this spicy little opener to jump-start the palate in the summer months. We slowly grill Mexican white shrimp seasoned with a hot and sweet green curry paste. Served atop a little bed of julienned cucumbers and green onion, finished with a small drop of mango crème fraîche, this is also a great lunch item when accompanied by short-grain sticky rice and a cold Asian-style beer.

You'll have more curry paste than you need, but it will keep well in the refrigerator for about a week and you'll appreciate its versatility as a baste or marinade for seafood or chicken.

RICE VINEGAR CUCUMBERS

1 tablespoon minced green onion

$1/2$ cup rice vinegar

$1/4$ cup sugar

2 tablespoons honey

2 teaspoons kosher salt

1 cup peeled, seeded, and julienned cucumber

MANGO CRÈME FRAÎCHE

2 tablespoons ripe mango purée

2 tablespoons crème fraîche (page 206)

Pinch of salt

Dash of freshly squeezed lemon juice

GREEN CURRY PASTE

1 teaspoon ground cinnamon

2 teaspoons cayenne pepper

2 tablespoons ground coriander

1 teaspoon ground cumin

1 teaspoon ground anise seed

1 teaspoon ground fenugreek seed

1 teaspoon ground turmeric

1 cup cilantro leaves

$1/2$ cup fresh Italian parsley leaves

2 tablespoons minced fresh ginger

1 tablespoon honey

$1/2$ cup coconut milk

$1^1/2$ cups light olive oil

1 tablespoon kosher salt

8 medium shrimp, peeled and deveined

1 tablespoon canola oil

Pinch of sea salt

4 small sprigs cilantro, for garnish

To prepare the cucumber salad, combine the green onion, vinegar, sugar, honey, and salt in a bowl and whisk until the sugar dissolves. Add the cucumber, and toss gently to coat. Cover and set aside in the refrigerator for 1 hour to macerate.

To prepare the mango crème fraîche, fold the mango purée and crème fraîche together in a bowl, and mix in the salt and lemon juice. Cover and refrigerate until ready to serve.

To prepare the curry paste, combine the cinnamon, cayenne, coriander, cumin, anise seed, fenugreek, and turmeric in a small bowl. In a food processor, purée the cilantro, parsley, ginger, honey, coconut milk, olive oil, and salt into a paste. Add the mixed dry spices, and blend well.

Prepare a medium fire in a charcoal grill, or preheat a gas grill to medium.

In a small bowl, lightly toss the shrimp with the oil and sea salt. Measure 2 tablespoons of the curry paste into a small, separate bowl. Gently lay each shrimp on the grill rack and cook, turning once, for about 30 seconds on each side. Put the partially cooked shrimp into the bowl with the curry paste, turning each shrimp to coat. Return the shrimp to the grill and cook for 1 minute on each side, until the shrimp is firm but not overcooked.

To assemble the dish, remove the cucumber salad from the refrigerator, and drain off any excess marinade. Divide the salad evenly among 4 small plates. Top each with 2 shrimp and a dollop of the mango crème fraîche. Garnish with a sprig of cilantro. Serve immediately.

Chive-Tied Bay Scallops with Black Truffle and Fresh Tomato Coulis

Serves 6

Our local fishmonger, Jeff Koscomb of Above Sea Level (see page 200), had sourced the sweetest little freshly shucked bay scallops from Mexico. Mexican bay scallops? I asked, incredulous. Aren't they just known for their Calicos? I'm kind of partial to the northern East Coast for scallops. Most of the time, we get our fresh sea scallops and bay scallops from Maine or other boutique fisheries thereabouts. However, he sent me a sample, and I was wowed! For this amuse, we tie a few bay scallops with a blanched chive, creating a sort of "tournedo," which is then poached lightly in a court-bouillon and Chablis just long enough to warm the little guys. We place them in a bright pool of fresh tomato coulis and add the great earthy taste of truffle. It's a mite tricky tying the scallops, especially if your fingers resemble plump sausages, as mine do. You can make these without tying the scallops if it seems daunting. You will need a 2-inch ring mold for preparing the scallop bundles.

1 black summer truffle

6 cups water

1 tablespoon kosher salt

15 chives, 10 inches long

48 fresh bay scallops (approximately 8 ounces)

TOMATO COULIS

2 tablespoons extra virgin olive oil

1 clove garlic, minced

2 tablespoons diced white onion

2 ripe Roma tomatoes, peeled (see page 219) and seeded

1 teaspoon capers

1 teaspoon minced fresh basil

Pinch of ground cinnamon

Pinch of salt

Pinch of freshly ground black pepper

2 tablespoons heavy cream

WILTED SPINACH

1 tablespoon unsalted butter

4 cups baby spinach, washed and stemmed

Pinch of sea salt

Pinch of freshly ground white pepper

1 tablespoon unsalted butter, at room temperature

1 shallot, thinly sliced

2 cups court-bouillon (page 214)

1 cup dry Chablis or any dry white wine

Sea salt

1 tablespoon truffle oil

Using a truffle slicer or mandoline, slice the truffle into 48 paper-thin circles. Using a 3/4-inch round cookie cutter, trim them into uniform 1/2-inch circles. Save the truffle scraps for another use; I always put them in a little Cognac or oil and refrigerate.

Pour the water into a saucepan, add the salt, and bring to a boil over medium-high heat. Fill a bowl with ice water. Blanch the chives in the boiling water for 10 seconds. Using a slotted spoon or strainer, transfer to the ice water bath. Shock for about 1 minute, or until thoroughly chilled. Immediately transfer the chives to a colander and drain. Using paper towels, gently press out all the water.

Dry the scallops thoroughly. Pack 8 of the scallops, side by side, inside a 2-inch ring mold. Press down gently. Lift off the ring mold and gently tie

one of the blanched chive strands around the scallops, encircling them twice if possible, and make a knot. Do not pull the chive strand too tight or it will break. Repeat the process 5 more times, and place the scallop bundles in a dish. Cover and refrigerate while preparing the coulis and the spinach.

To make the tomato coulis, heat the olive oil in a saucepan over medium-high heat. Add the garlic and onion, and sauté for about 2 minutes, or until translucent. Add the tomatoes, capers, basil, cinnamon, salt, pepper, and cream and sauté for about 2 minutes longer. Remove from the heat and transfer to a blender. Purée until smooth. Be careful that the lid is tightly secured on the blender when puréeing: steam will be produced and can pop the lid. Set the coulis aside in a warm spot.

To prepare the spinach, melt the butter in a sauté pan over medium heat, and let it turn slightly golden brown. Add the spinach, salt, and pepper and cook for about 1 minute, until tender. Drain in a colander. Set aside in a warm place.

To cook the scallops, brush the butter on the bottom of a 10-inch flat saucepan. Lay the slices of shallot in the butter. Gently set the 6 scallop bundles, spaced evenly, in the pan. Cover with the court-bouillon and wine, and add a few pinches of sea salt. Cover and place over medium-high heat. Bring to a simmer, then decrease the heat to low and cook for about 3 minutes. To preserve their soft, sweet texture, the scallops should not be cooked through. Even fresh scallops will turn rubbery if overcooked.

Remove from the heat, take off the lid, and insert the discs of sliced truffle between the scallops. Sprinkle each one with a few drops of truffle oil.

To assemble, place a spoonful of the tomato coulis into the center of 6 small, shallow bowls. Divide the spinach equally into 6 mounds, set one mound in each bowl, and place a scallop bundle directly atop the spinach. Serve immediately.

Chicken "Oysters" with Smoked Apple-Thyme Jus in Bouchées

Serves 8

When roasting a whole chicken, you may have noticed the two small pieces of meat underneath the bird that fill two tiny pockets where the backbone meets the thighs. At home, it's always a loving little gesture to offer the oysters to another. These tender morsels are simply divine. After we roast a bunch of birds, we gently remove the two oysters from the carcasses and make this great amuse. We make bouchées, which are buttery little puff pastry cups, fill them with the chicken oysters and a dollop of apple purée, and finish them with a spoonful of smoky apple-thyme jus. The jus recipe will make enough for a whole dinner party, to serve with roasted chicken, if desired. It will keep for about a week if properly cooled and refrigerated.

APPLE-THYME JUS

1 tablespoon light olive oil

1/4 cup diced smoked bacon

2 Granny Smith apples, peeled, cored, and diced

1/2 cup diced leek, rinsed well, white part only

1/2 cup diced celery

1 teaspoon tomato paste

1 pinch ground cloves

1 bay leaf

2 sprigs thyme

4 black peppercorns

1 cup apple juice

1 tablespoon balsamic vinegar

1 tablespoon apple cider vinegar

1 cup veal demi-glace (page 212)

1 cup blonde chicken stock (page 213)

APPLE PURÉE

1 tablespoon unsalted butter

1 cup peeled, cored, seeded, and diced Granny Smith apple

1 pinch ground cinnamon

1 pinch freshly ground white pepper

1 tablespoon brown sugar

1 cup apple juice

1/4 teaspoon freshly squeezed lemon juice

Pinch of salt

8 bouchées (page 205)

16 roasted chicken oysters

1 Granny Smith apple, julienned (skin on), for garnish

8 sprigs thyme, for garnish

To prepare the jus, heat the olive oil in a saucepan over medium heat. Add the bacon and sauté for about 3 minutes, until it begins to brown. Add the apples, leeks, and celery and sauté for 1 minute. Add the tomato paste and stir with a wooden spoon for 5 minutes, until the tomato paste begins to brown slightly. Add the cloves, bay leaf, thyme, peppercorns, apple juice, balsamic vinegar, apple cider vinegar, demi-glace, and chicken stock. Decrease the heat to low and simmer for about 35 minutes, until all the vegetables are softened. Pass through a chinois into a clean saucepan, pressing down firmly on the solids to extract all the liquid. Discard the solids.

Return the liquid to the stove over medium-low heat, and simmer for about 10 minutes, until reduced by half. Remove from the heat and keep warm.

To prepare the purée, place the butter in a sauté pan over medium heat. When the butter is slightly browned, add the apples and sauté for about 2 minutes, until softened. Stir in the cinnamon, white pepper, sugar, apple juice, lemon juice, and salt and decrease the heat to low. Cover and simmer for about 10 minutes, until the apples are fully cooked. Transfer the apple mixture to a blender or food processor, and process until smooth.

To serve, warm 8 small plates in the oven, arrange the bouchées on them, and set aside.

In a sauté pan over medium heat, gently combine the chicken and $1/2$ cup of the jus and bring just to a simmer. Decrease the heat to low.

Place a bouchée on each of the warmed plates.

With a teaspoon, place a dollop of the apple purée in each bouchée, and top each with 2 pieces of chicken. Drizzle with a scant spoonful of the jus. Garnish each serving with julienned apple and a sprig of thyme. Serve immediately.

At nineteen I made the decision to go into the restaurant business. I knew I loved it. Knew I could be and would be good at it, knew I had something to offer. There was no question in my mind. None.

Cliff on . . . My Beginnings: Un, Deux, Trois

I had never waited tables before, never served a cocktail before. I walked into Café Un Deux Trois, between Sixth and Broadway, because I'd heard it was really busy, thinking, I'm going to get a job here.

I had just moved from Utah to New York City two or three days before. It was midmorning, before lunch, around ten, ten thirty. I walked up and told the bartender I wanted to apply for a job. He said, "Well, we need a lunch waiter right now," adding, "I'm the assistant manager. I manage lunch, so if you would like to fill out an application . . ."

He asked me how much experience I had. I answered that I'd worked in a few places out on the West Coast, that I was definitely a quick learner, and that I'd do whatever was needed to get the job. I told him, if you give me the job, I can promise you, I will not disappoint you.

He hired me on the spot, saying, "Show up tomorrow in black pants, a white shirt and a bow tie." I took the lunch menu home and memorized it. It was brasserie-type French food; whatever I wasn't familiar with, I looked up in a book I had bought on French cuisine. And I showed up, a little nervous, but excited.

There was one little glitch in the whole thing, and that was the bar. I knew absolutely not a thing about mixed drinks. Nothing.

The first table that I went up to, I had started taking the food order, when the man piped up, "I'll have an Absolut and tonic with a squeeze of lime, all right?" I carefully wrote down "Absolutely. Tonic." I went immediately to the bartender and said with authority, "Absolutely tonic and a squeeze of lime." The bartender laughed, "You don't know anything about alcohol, do you?" I answered, "Well, he said 'Absolutely,' 'Absolutely tonic.'" The bartender cracked up, saying, "Okay, it's Absolut and tonic with a squeeze of lime."

At my next table, the man ordered "Glenfiddich, neat." And again I marched up to the bartender, this time with a big grin, "Glen Bibbitch. He wants us to make it really neat. Glen Bibbitch. Neat. I don't know." The bartender just roared with laughter.

I immediately went out, bought more books, and started reading them. I was determined to learn those drinks!

Eventually, I got it. Every day I'd come to work hours before my shift began, because I wanted to know everything about the restaurant. I'd follow people around. I went into the kitchen. I wanted to know where they stored things. I wanted to know how it all worked.

In four months, the owners came to me and asked me to become the assistant manager. I started waiting tables at night and being assistant manager during the day. Two months later the general manager left, and I was invited to take that position, six months after walking in off the street.

During the next few years at Un Deux Trois, I got to know the business really well. Being the maître d' was part of my job, and I quickly learned that the guy with the short, croppy white hair, and white pasty skin, who always showed up in a limousine, *always* got a table. "Right this way Mr. Warhol," I'd say, smiling.

In learned the ins and outs, the ups and downs, the finesse of seating 400 people a night without reservations: whom to seat when, whom to seat where, and who Liliane Montevecchi was. As far as I know, the staff's longstanding bets about those huge hats of hers are still on . . .

Then it came time to make the next move. There was buzz on the street about a hot, upscale restaurant about to open in the city. To my great pleasure and surprise, the owners of this new place approached me, saying, "You must come and work with us." I thought, Oooh, this is scary! I'm going to have to wear a suit and tie. I knew that to take the next step in the real restaurant world I had to do this. So I accepted. And indeed, it was a whole different scene.

It was hard-core. It was cutthroat. It was art, it was who's who, who's doing what with whom, Gael Greene, and reviews, and it was all about the detail. Everything possible was done to ensure that the customer's desires were fulfilled.

A woman might say, "I'd like the T-bone." I'd rush back to the kitchen, and say worriedly, "Chef, she wants the T-bone! We're out of that!" He would say, "That's okay. I'll fix it." He'd prepare salmon. Then he'd personally bring out the salmon and tell her, "You know, I just made this dish. It's not on the menu. And I wanted to make it for *you*." Invariably, she would flush happily and exclaim, "Oh, that's so wonderful of you to do that!"

Or, someone might ask for a glass of rosé. We didn't serve rosé, but rather than say that, we would ask if, perhaps, they would like to try a beautiful Pinot Grigio, thinking that the sweetness of the wine would satisfy their taste for rosé, while also providing a more delicious beverage, and a finer accompaniment to the meal.

I learned to find the yes in the no, a way to turn a potentially awkward situation into something that enhanced the customer's pleasure, a lesson that has become the keystone of the Geronimo Experience.

Soups

Spring Asparagus Soup with Crispy Prosciutto

Serves 6

In springtime come baskets of fresh asparagus, vivid green, white, even purple. Even though we use asparagus year round at Geronimo, in the spring months, their flavor evokes the season: crisp, newly warming Santa Fe air, streams rushing full with snowmelt, and of course, the celebratory opening of our local farmers' market.

This recipe is very simple, and really tastes like asparagus. That may sound funny, but the pleasure of this soup resides in the fact that we don't adulterate it with a lot of spice; we let the true flavor of the asparagus dominate, simmered in the flavorful blonde chicken stock and then finishing the silken soup with sweet butter, crème fraîche, and crispy prosciutto lardons.

$1/2$ cup unsalted butter

$1/2$ cup diced yellow onion

2 tablespoons thinly sliced shallot

12 cups blonde chicken stock (page 213)

8 cups coarsely chopped asparagus, stems and all (about 20 spears)

$1/2$ cup chopped fresh Italian parsley

3 thin slices prosciutto

ASPARAGUS GARNISH

8 cups water

2 tablespoons kosher salt

24 asparagus spears, peeled and cut into 3-inch pieces

1 cup blonde chicken stock (page 213)

2 cups crème fraîche (page 206)

Sea salt

$1/2$ teaspoon freshly ground white pepper

In a large soup pot over medium heat, melt $1/4$ cup of the butter. Add the onion and shallot and sauté for about 2 minutes, until slightly brown. Add the chicken stock and bring to a simmer. Add the asparagus and parsley and cook for about 5 minutes, until very tender but still green and vibrant. Use a handheld immersion blender to purée the vegetables in the pot, or purée them in small batches in a food processor or blender and then return the purée to the simmering stock.

Continue to cook for another 10 minutes, stirring to prevent the puréed vegetables from burning on the bottom of the pot.

Pass the soup through a chinois into a clean soup pot to extract the stringy asparagus stems and achieve a silky texture. Place the pot over medium heat and cook for 8 to 10 minutes, until the soup reduces to the desired consistency. Decrease the heat to low, and keep warm.

Place several layers of paper towels on a plate.

Place a large sauté pan over medium-high heat and, when hot, lay the slices of prosciutto in the pan. Cook for 1 to 2 minutes per side, until crisp on both sides, taking care not to burn them. Transfer to the paper towels to drain. Let cool for 5 minutes. Julienne the prosciutto and place on a dry paper towel.

To prepare the asparagus garnish, pour the water into a saucepan and add the salt. Bring to a boil over medium-high heat. Fill a bowl with ice water. Blanch the asparagus in the boiling water for about 2 minutes, until al dente. Using a slotted spoon or strainer, transfer the asparagus to the ice water bath. Shock for about 1 minute, until thoroughly chilled. Immediately transfer the asparagus to a colander and drain.

Place a sauté pan over medium heat and add the chicken stock. Add the asparagus and bring to a simmer. Simmer for 1 to 2 minutes, until heated through.

To finish the soup, whisk in the crème fraîche and the remaining 1/4 cup butter. Add salt to taste and the white pepper.

To serve, stand the blanched asparagus, spaced evenly apart, up against the inside of 6 soup bowls.

Pour the soup directly into the center of the bowls and garnish with the crispy prosciutto. Serve immediately.

Crab and Meyer Lemon Soup with Spaetzle

Serves 6 generously

I almost want to call this a chowder because it's so thick with diced celery, fennel, and onions. You will notice, however, that instead of potatoes, we make a spaetzle that adds a rich texture to this combination of vegetables and creamy broth. I love to use those sweet, sweet Maryland blue crabs for this soup. This recipe is lengthy, since everything is made from scratch. To make it easier to prepare, you could make the stock a day ahead and refrigerate the crabmeat for preparation the following day. If you make a big batch of the stock, freeze it, and buy fresh crabmeat, it will be very easy to make this soup. Large loaves of warm, crusty bread are a natural accompaniment.

SPAETZLE

$1^1/_2$ cups milk

$1/_3$ cup canola oil

1 egg

1 egg yolk

3 cups all-purpose flour

1 teaspoon salt

$1/_2$ teaspoon freshly ground nutmeg

CRAB STOCK AND CRABMEAT

1 yellow onion, diced

5 quarts water

1 cup malt vinegar

3 tablespoons crustacean spice (page 206)

1 lemon, cut in half

3 bay leaves

6 live blue crabs, or $1^1/_2$ pounds of crabmeat

SOUP

1 cup unsalted butter

$1/_2$ cup thinly sliced shallot

1 cup diced yellow onion

2 cups diced celery

1 cup fresh sweet corn kernels, from about 2 ears

1 cup diced fennel bulb

2 tablespoons minced garlic

$1/_2$ tablespoon crushed dried red chile flakes

2 jalapeños, seeded and minced

$1/_2$ teaspoon sugar

1 tablespoon crustacean spice (page 206)

1 cup all-purpose flour

Freshly squeezed juice of 2 Meyer lemons

2 cups heavy cream

$1/_2$ cup finely chopped fresh Italian parsley

Bring a large pot of salted water to a boil. Fill a large bowl with ice water.

To prepare the spaetzle, whisk together the milk, canola oil, egg, and egg yolk in a bowl. In a separate bowl, sift together the flour, salt, and nutmeg. Make a well in the flour, add the egg and milk mixture, and stir together until a batter forms. With a floured hand, beat the dough with a slapping motion for a few minutes. This makes the batter smooth and forms the necessary gluten to give the spaetzle its chewy texture. Place a large-holed colander over the boiling water, making sure there is a couple of inches of space between the colander and the water. Drop the dough into the colander and press the mixture through the holes with a spatula, letting the batter drop off into the water. After all the batter has been pressed through the holes, remove the colander, and gently stir the spaetzle. Boil for 1 or 2 minutes, until they rise to the top. Drain in a clean colander and transfer to the ice water to stop the cooking process.

Drain again, place in a bowl, cover, and refrigerate until needed.

To prepare the stock, in a soup pot, combine the onion, water, vinegar, crustacean spice, lemon, and bay leaves and bring to a boil over high heat. Drop in the crabs and cook for about 5 minutes, until the shells turn bright red. With a pair of tongs or a spider, remove the crabs from the liquid, and set aside to cool. Decrease the heat to medium and maintain the stock at a simmer.

When the crabs have cooled enough to handle, using a mallet and cracker, carefully break open the shells and dig out all the meat you can from the claws and body. Remove and discard the lungs or, as they're sometimes called, devil's horns, but keep all the cracked shells and legs. Place the crabmeat in a bowl, cover, and refrigerate.

Return all the shells to the stock, and simmer for 30 minutes. Strain the stock through a sturdy colander and press down on the shells to extract all the liquid. Discard the shells. Strain the stock one more time through a chinois into a clean soup pot, and keep it warm on the stove, over very low heat.

To prepare the soup, place a clean, large, heavy-bottomed soup pot over medium-low heat. Melt the butter in the pot and cook until slightly brown. Add the shallot, onion, 1 cup of the celery, corn, fennel, garlic, chile flakes, jalapeños, sugar, and crustacean spice and sauté for about 2 minutes, until the celery and onion begin to soften. Add the flour and stir with a wooden spoon until it is incorporated with the butter. Decrease the heat to low and cook, stirring frequently, for about 5 minutes, until the mixture is bubbling. This makes the roux that thickens the soup. Turn off the heat.

Add the crab stock to the roux and whisk until smooth. Turn the heat on to medium-low and bring the soup to a simmer, stirring occasionally so that nothing sticks to the bottom. Skim off any impurities as they rise to the top, and cook for about 20 minutes. Add the crabmeat, spaetzle, the remaining 1 cup of celery, lemon juice, and cream. Cook for another 5 minutes, stir in the parsley, and check for seasoning. Ladle into deep bowls and serve immediately.

Braised Celery Soup with Mini-Manicotti Stuffed with Celery Purée and Fresh Ricotta Cheese

Serves 6

This recipe comes from my days as a saucier at the Hotel Hershey, where we made the stock in giant steam kettle stockpots that you could boil a whole cow in, or turn the heat down, and have a Jacuzzi for yourself and four friends. As the saucier, I used these kettles to make large batches of all varieties of stock. For this recipe, we use both our "blonde" and our roasted, or "brown," chicken stock. To make that stock, we would roast the chicken bones, chicken necks, and feet until golden brown, and use a white mire poix: lots of onions, leeks, herbs, and, of course, celery—no tomato influence at all. I worked in the back of the kitchen with a short little vegetable prep man named Jim Burger. After about four hours of simmering and skimming, we would strain the stock, leaving a big pile of bones and overcooked vegetables. Then, like clockwork, Jim would mosey over to the pile, pick out big chunks of celery, salt, pepper, and butter them, and go to town. I dedicate this soup to the memory of Jim Burger, who showed me a delicacy in an old stockpot.

If you don't use fresh ricotta, drain the excess liquid from the cheese overnight in the refrigerator, in a sieve lined with cheesecloth. Also note that the pasta dough will need to rest for 1 hour before you make the manicotti.

MINI-MANICOTTI

2 tablespoons unsalted butter

2 cups diced celery hearts

1 clove garlic, minced

1 shallot, minced

1/2 teaspoon kosher salt

1 cup blonde chicken stock (page 213)

1 teaspoon freshly ground celery seed

2 cups fresh ricotta cheese

Pinch of freshly ground nutmeg

2 eggs, whisked

1 recipe pasta dough (page 210)

EGG WASH

4 egg yolks

1 teaspoon cold water

BRAISED CELERY SOUP

1/2 cup unsalted butter

15 young celery stalks, coarsely chopped, about 8 cups

1 cup diced yellow onion

1 cup diced leek

1/2 cup sliced shallot

1 cup long-grain white rice

2 tablespoons celery seed

1 teaspoon freshly ground white pepper

12 cups brown chicken stock (page 214)

2 cups heavy cream

2 tablespoons parsley paste (page 210)

Kosher salt

2 cups blonde chicken stock (page 213)

Celery leaves, for garnish

2-inch chive sticks, for garnish

To prepare the mini-manicotti, melt the butter in a large sauté pan over medium heat. Add the celery hearts, garlic, shallot, and salt and sauté for about 5 minutes, until the vegetables become translucent. Add the chicken stock and ground celery seed, and simmer for about 10 minutes, until the vegetables

are tender. Transfer to a food processor and blend until smooth. To remove any stringiness from the celery and onions, push through a tamis or fine-mesh sieve into a bowl. Set the bowl over an ice water bath. When the mixture has cooled, add the ricotta cheese and nutmeg and fold together. Add the eggs and mix well. Cover and refrigerate.

Roll the pasta dough out onto a lightly floured surface to about $1/16$ inch thick, or use the ravioli setting on a pasta machine. The pasta dough should be thin, but not so thin that it will dry out or tear easily when making the manicotti. Cut the pasta sheets into 54 (2 by 3-inch) rectangles. Keep the pasta that you're not working with covered with a damp towel.

Make the egg wash by whisking the egg yolks with the cold water in a small bowl. On a lightly floured surface, arrange 5 to 8 of the pasta rectangles. With a small pastry brush, brush one of the 2-inch edges with egg wash. Distribute 1 teaspoon of the celery-cheese mixture along the opposite edge and, working from the filling side, roll toward the egg-washed side. Press very gently to seal the edge, creating a cigarlike shape. As you make them, set the manicotti on a baking sheet and cover with a damp towel. When all the manicotti are made, place in the refrigerator while making the soup.

To prepare the soup, melt the butter in a large soup pot over low heat, and add the celery, onion, leek, shallot, rice, celery seed, and white pepper. Sauté over low heat for about 5 minutes, until the onions are translucent. Add the brown stock, bring to a simmer, and simmer for about 15 minutes over medium heat, until the rice is fully cooked and the celery is very tender. Using a hand-held immersion blender or transferring the soup to a blender, purée the soup until smooth. Return to the pot, add the cream, parsley paste, and salt to taste, and stir well. Keep hot over low heat.

Drizzle a little olive oil into the bottom of a flameproof baking dish with sides. Arrange the manicotti in the dish. Pour the blonde chicken stock over the manicotti and cover with aluminum foil, making sure the foil does not touch the manicotti. Place over low heat. This creates a steamer of sorts; if you have a bamboo steamer and a wok, that would also work well. Steam the manicotti for about 5 minutes, until the pasta is al dente.

For best presentation, stack 9 manicotti in each soup bowl and garnish with celery leaves and chives. Pour the soup into a tureen, and ladle it into the bowls at the table.

English Cotswold Cheddar and Cauliflower Bisque

Serves 6

Comfort, comfort, comfort! This combination of tangy English cheddar and delicate cauliflower, with a hint of beer, is a great winter soup. English cheddars are truly some of the best, and Cotswold is one that, once tasted, is truly memorable and will certainly become a part of your cheese repertoire. I also love Vermont cheddars; they would also work beautifully in this recipe. Obviously, this is a rich soup and would go well with a light salad. This soup does not reheat well because of all the cheese.

CHEDDAR AND CAULIFLOWER BISQUE

3 tablespoons unsalted butter

1 cup very finely diced yellow onion

3 tablespoons all-purpose flour

4 cups whole milk

4 cups brown chicken stock (page 214)

1 bottle (12 ounces) dark beer (we use Negra Modelo)

1 bouquet garni (page 205)

2 cups cauliflower florets

1 serrano chile, seeded and minced

1¾ cups crumbled English Cotswold cheddar cheese

CROUTONS

6 thick slices French baguette, cut on the diagonal

2 tablespoons unsalted butter

½ teaspoon minced garlic

½ teaspoon freshly cracked black pepper

¼ cup crumbled English Cotswold cheddar cheese, for garnish

2 tablespoons minced fresh chives, for garnish

In a heavy-bottomed soup pot, melt the butter over medium heat. Add the onion and stir for about 5 minutes, until the onion is golden but not brown. Add the flour and stir until bubbling. Whisk in the milk, stock, and beer, and bring to a slow boil. Add the bouquet garni, cauliflower, and chile and simmer for about 15 minutes, until the cauliflower is tender. Skim off any impurities that rise to the top. Pull the pot to one side of the heat, so that the impurities rise to one side, making them easier to skim off with a ladle.

Preheat the oven to 450°F.

Remove the cauliflower and bouquet garni from the soup with a slotted spoon. Discard the bouquet garni. Purée the cauliflower in a food processor until smooth, then return to the soup pot. Turn off the heat, stir in the cheese, and set aside in a warm place.

To prepare the croutons, butter one side of each bread slice, sprinkle with the garlic and cracked pepper, and bake on a baking sheet for about 10 minutes, until golden brown.

Ladle the soup into 6 bowls and place a warm crouton at a slant in each bowl, leaving one end visible. Generously sprinkle the cheese and chives atop the soup, and serve immediately.

Brie and Almond Soup

For me, Brie and almonds go together like caviar and Champagne. The richness of this fondue-like soup, coupled with the toasted almond butter and wine, really captures a wonderfully romantic by-the-fire cheese moment. We add a little cayenne pepper to give it a bit of a kick. This soup would be excellent with toasted, smoked ham sandwiches spread with a bit of Creole mustard. However, just enjoying this soup with generous slices of oven-warmed, crusty sourdough bread and a Guinness is also very fine.

1¼ cups whole, unsalted, blanched almonds, toasted (page 219)

1 pound triple-cream Brie cheese

3 cups white wine

3 cups blonde chicken stock (page 213)

1 cup whole milk

1 tablespoon cornstarch

1 tablespoon water

½ teaspoon cayenne pepper

Sea salt

2 tablespoons minced chives, for garnish

Preheat the oven to 400°F.

Place the toasted almonds in a food processor and, using the metal blade, purée them to a thick paste.

Cut the Brie into 1-inch by 1-inch cubes. Cover and set aside at room temperature.

In a heavy-bottomed soup pot over medium heat, combine the wine, stock, and milk. Bring to a simmer and cook for 15 minutes. In a separate small bowl, whisk the cornstarch and water together until smooth.

Whisk the cornstarch mixture into the soup base, and continue whisking until no sign of the starch is visible.

Decrease the heat to low, and simmer the soup for about 5 minutes, skimming off the impurities as necessary. Add the Brie, almond butter, and cayenne pepper. Stir constantly with a wooden spoon until all the cheese is melted.

Strain the soup through a medium-mesh sieve, compressing the Brie rind to push out all the cheese. Add sea salt to taste, and sprinkle the chives over the top.

Serve immediately, ladling the soup into bowls.

White Truffle Egg Drop Soup

Serves 6

I have always loved egg drop soup. When I was a boy, my mother would make it for me when I was sick, and I used to just hunger after it. She would crack eggs, whip them with Parmesan or Romano cheese, and stir them into the simmering chicken broth. They would become so fluffy, and they made an excellent marriage with the flavorful chicken stock.

At Geronimo, a hint of white truffle oil to the rich, piping hot broth, which is actually a double stock. Then we toss in a fresh julienne of romaine hearts, add aged Asiago and grated Parmigiano-Reggiano to the eggs, and finish the whole bowl with some sliced fresh white truffle.

It's very important to serve this soup immediately after you've added the egg mixture, to appreciate the visual effect: bountiful clouds of cheese and egg. The fresh white truffle is optional, because they are very seasonal and very expensive. If you leave them out, add a few drops more of the white truffle oil.

SOUP

1 good-quality chicken, 3 pounds

1 gallon blonde chicken stock (page 213)

2 stalks celery

1 medium yellow onion, diced

1 shallot, minced

1 bay leaf

2 sprigs thyme

2 tablespoons white truffle oil

EGG FINISH

8 eggs

4 egg yolks

2 cups grated Asiago cheese

2 cups grated Parmigiano-Reggiano cheese

$^1/_2$ cup minced fresh chives

3 cups julienned romaine hearts, for garnish

1 white truffle, for garnish (optional)

Fill a large pot, one that will easily hold your whole chicken, halfway with salted water, place over high heat, and bring to a boil. Carefully slip the whole chicken into the boiling water, and let it sit for about 3 minutes; the chicken should be completely covered by the water.

Remove the chicken from the pot, and thoroughly rinse the bird with cold water. Place it in another pot of the same size, or clean and reuse the same pot. This step pulls out the impurities from the chicken, so they don't affect the clarity or flavor of the stock. Add the chicken stock to the pot. Make sure the bird is covered by at least 2 inches of stock; add more stock if necessary. Add the celery, onion, shallot, bay leaf, and thyme. Bring the soup to a light boil over medium-high heat, then decrease the heat and simmer for 1 hour, or until it thickens slightly. It is important that it be just at a simmer, because a rolling boil will evaporate your stock prematurely and will make it cloudy. After an hour of simmering, remove the chicken and set it aside in a colander, over a bowl.

For extra clarity, strain the remaining stock and vegetables through a fine-mesh sieve into a smaller soup pot. Simmer over low heat for another 20 minutes, skimming off any impurities and chicken fat. At this point, pour in the white truffle oil. Check the seasoning, and set aside in a warm place.

To finish the soup, with an electric mixer fitted with a whip attachment, whip the eggs and yolks together in a mixing bowl until they are very fluffy. Add the cheeses and chives, and whip for another minute. Leave the egg mixture in the mixer, because you are going to mix it one more time before adding it to the soup.

Prepare 6 shallow bowls with a nest of romaine in the center of each. Using a truffle slicer, liberally shave the white truffle over each bed of lettuce.

Over medium heat, bring the soup up to a nice simmer.

Whip the egg mixture for 1 minute, and then slowly pour it into the soup and let it rise to the top. Stir it one time with a spoon, to break up the raft of eggs, and turn off the heat. For the best presentation, serve the soup in a large terrine, and ladle it out at the table.

Champagne and Scallop Soup with Crème Fraîche

Serves 6

I've always kept this soup in my repertoire because it's both simple and opulent and is just so good. Somehow, no matter how much of this soup you make, it never seems to be enough. It's not hard to make, but cooking the scallops à point and finishing the soup with Champagne at the end are crucial steps. As with any soup or sauce, starting out with a good stock is important. This creamy soup goes beautifully with a light rocket salad and some soft, warm potato rolls.

SCALLOPS

2 tablespoons unsalted butter

2 pounds fresh bay scallops

Pinch of sea salt

Pinch of freshly ground white pepper

SOUP

1/2 cup unsalted butter

1/2 cup finely minced yellow onion

1/2 cup minced shallot

1/2 teaspoon finely minced garlic

1/4 cup minced celery

2 tablespoons fresh thyme leaves in a sachet

2 cups dry white wine

4 cups fish stock (page 215)

2 cups heavy cream

Sea salt

Freshly ground white pepper

2 cups Champagne (at room temperature)

2 tablespoons finely chopped Italian parsley leaves

Crème fraîche (page 206)

To prepare the scallops, place a large sauté pan over low heat, add the butter and let it melt, being careful not to brown. Add the scallops, season with the salt and white pepper, and sauté for about 2 minutes. Remove from the heat and set aside.

To prepare the soup, set a heavy-bottomed soup pot over medium heat. For this soup, I use a ceramic-coated pot, because I don't want any browning to occur in the cooking process. Add the butter, onion, shallot, garlic, celery, and thyme sachet, and sauté until the onion becomes translucent. Add the white wine, fish stock, and heavy cream. Bring to a simmer. Decrease the heat to medium-low and skim off the impurities as they rise to the top.

Cook for about 30 minutes, or longer if a thicker, more intense soup is desired. Add salt and white pepper to taste. Remove from the heat. Strain through a fine-mesh sieve into a clean soup pot. Return to low heat and keep hot.

Add the sautéed scallops, Champagne, and chopped parsley to the soup. Ladle into 6 bowls, and top each with a dollop of crème fraîche. Serve immediately.

When my father died, I was in my twenties, living in New York, a general manager and partner running three major restaurants in New York City and one in London. I flew to Las Vegas for his funeral. Sensing that fresh scenery would do my mother and me some good, I decided we should take a drive to Santa Fe; we both had always wanted to visit there.

Several New York restaurateurs whom I respected had recently announced, out of the blue, that they were moving to Santa Fe. I thought it was very cool that they were willing to give up all they had in New York and break away into something new.

All I knew about Santa Fe was what I had read, including an intriguing description of a restaurant called Alfonso's, on a street called Canyon Road.

On our first morning we drove up Canyon Road, past galleries and lush gardens, pulled into the parking lot of Alfonso's and walked in. I instantly got goose bumps. What an incredible building! What a sensational place!

We went into the back dining room, sat down at what are now the cocktail tables in our bar. I had green chile stew with my mother, and it was fantastic. The feel of the room was extraordinary.

I vividly remember thinking, "This is the most marvelous place." My mother and I joked and laughed about it, and I said to her, "You know, if I could possibly have anything, anything, I wanted, it would be to live in this town and to own this building."

"Cliff," she replied, "If it's really something you want to do, I know you will."

Pulling out of the parking lot looking over my shoulder, I wondered to myself, how and when I would find my way back here.

Cliff on . . . Love at First Sight

First Courses

Seared Foie Gras with Fresh Berries, Caramelized Maui Pineapple, Amish Apple Butter, and Port Wine Reduction

Serves 4

Foie gras is one of the most succulent and decadent of foodstuffs. I can never resist a slice of it, served warm with fresh fruit, especially Maui pineapple, marrying the juicy tang of sweet fruit with the sensuously rich liver. To ensure a good result with this recipe, purchase the foie gras from an experienced purveyor, and have it deveined and trimmed.

The apple butter in this dish comes from an Amish recipe recollected from my childhood, growing up near Lancaster, Pennsylvania. During the apple harvest season, the small orchard homesteads produce an abundance of apple products using the local provender, mostly Braeburn and Golden Delicious. I prefer Granny Smiths for this recipe because they are nice and tart and cook down beautifully. They are one of my favorite apples.

We'd buy dense, rustic Amish bread and slather warm apple butter on the thick slices. You'll have enough extra to enjoy that pleasure yourself, and the butter keeps well for several days in the refrigerator, or it may be canned.

APPLE BUTTER

6 pounds Granny Smith apples, peeled, cored, halved, and cubed

2 1/2 cups fresh apple cider

2 cups firmly packed light brown sugar

2 tablespoons grated lemon zest

1 tablespoon ground cinnamon

1 teaspoon ground allspice

1/2 teaspoon ground cloves

1/2 teaspoon freshly grated nutmeg

1/2 teaspoon salt

2 cups port wine

1 lobe foie gras, about 1 pound, deveined and trimmed

1 Maui pineapple

2 tablespoons superfine sugar

1 cup ripe, fresh blackberries or raspberries

1/4 cup slivered almonds, toasted (page 219)

4 pinches of fleur de sel or kosher salt

Freshly ground black pepper

4 sprigs of fresh mint, for garnish

Preheat the oven to 325°F.

To prepare the apple butter, place the apples, cider, brown sugar, lemon zest, cinnamon, allspice, cloves, nutmeg, and salt in a covered Dutch oven or a large, heavy-bottomed, ovenproof saucepan with a tight-fitting lid. Place in the oven and cook for 1 hour, until the apples are completely soft. Remove from the oven and transfer the mixture to a food processor. Purée until very smooth. To achieve a silkier, more refined texture, press the mixture through a tamis into a bowl, pushing it through with a rubber spatula. Cover and set aside.

To prepare the port wine reduction, place a saucepan over medium heat and pour in the port. Simmer at a very low boil for about 10 minutes, until the wine is reduced to about 1/4 cup. Remove from the heat.

To prepare the foie gras, soak the blade of a thin, sharp knife in warm water, and wipe dry. With the warm blade, carefully slice the foie gras into 4 equal slices. Using a piece of wax paper as a covering, gently press each slice with the palms of your hands to create a nicely uniform piece with a searable, flat surface. Foie gras is totally pliable and forgiving; you can press together any miscut pieces and make any shapes you need. Lay the slices flat on a plate. With a very sharp, warmed knife, lightly score the surface of the slices with a crosshatch pattern. Cover gently with plastic wrap and refrigerate. Chill thoroughly until ready for use.

To prepare the pineapple, use a serrated knife to cut off both ends, and then slice away the spiny skin. Halve the pineapple lengthwise, and set one half aside for another use. Remove the core from the other half and halve it again. Slice the quartered pineapple into 12 slices, $1/3$ inch thick. Sprinkle the sugar evenly over both sides of each slice.

Set out 4 salad plates.

Place a large nonstick sauté pan over medium-high heat. When the pan is hot, arrange the sugared pineapple slices in the pan and caramelize them, heating the sugar for about 1 minute, until it liquefies and turns golden. Turn the slices over, and caramelize the other side. Remove from the heat. Transfer 3 slices of the pineapple into the center of each plate.

In a small bowl, gently toss the berries and almonds with half of the port wine reduction.

To finish, place a large cast iron skillet over medium heat until very hot. While the pan comes to temperature, carefully arrange the berries and almonds over the pineapple slices. Place a dollop of apple butter on top.

Remove the foie gras from the refrigerator and season with the salt and pepper. Gently lay the pieces in the dry, hot pan, and sear for 45 seconds per side, just until brown and crispy. Remove from the heat. Quickly and carefully transfer the slices of foie to the plates, laying a piece atop each mound of fruit. Circle the foie with a drizzle of the remaining port reduction. Serve immediately.

Pan-Braised Veal Sweetbreads with Savory Green Apple Polenta

Serves 4

Here's a comical story, involving sweetbreads and a good friend of mine, Lester Deimler, the food controller at the Hotel Hershey. Amazing at his job, he was able to find foodstuffs that nobody else could. One day, for some reason, we were shorted sweetbreads by our veal guy, and we needed a few orders of them for a special party that night. So, scrambling, Lester got in touch with a local supermarket, and found some. He sent his assistant, recently promoted from errand boy, down to get them, and the man returned with a huge bag, crammed with bread loaves packaged in colorful Hawaiian luau paper. All I can remember, before being bent over laughing hysterically, was Lester asking his assistant, "What the hell are these for?!?" The reply: "That's the only sweet bread they had!"

We still have our share of diners who ask, "What are sweetbreads?" They are the thymus glands of animals. We use the sweetbreads from milk-fed veal. They are in two parts: the top, called the heart, and the bottom, called the lobe. The heart is the most desirable of the two and needs to be ordered from your butcher. Start preparing this recipe 24 hours in advance of serving.

1¹/₂ pounds "heart" sweetbreads

¹/₂ lobe (8 ounces) foie gras, deveined and trimmed

12 cups blonde chicken stock (page 213)

4 cups fresh apple cider

GREEN APPLE POLENTA

2 tablespoons unsalted butter

2 tablespoons minced shallot

¹/₄ teaspoon minced garlic

1 tablespoon minced fresh savory

1 cup peeled, cored, and diced Granny Smith apple

¹/₂ cup water

1 cup half-and-half

¹/₄ cup white cornmeal

¹/₄ cup grated Parmigiano-Reggiano cheese

Kosher salt

Freshly ground white pepper

Kosher salt

Freshly ground white pepper

¹/₂ cup all-purpose flour

¹/₄ cup canola oil

¹/₂ cup julienned Granny Smith apples, for garnish

To prepare the sweetbreads, fill a large bowl with ice water, add the sweetbreads, and soak them for 4 hours. Drain in a colander placed in the sink, refill the bowl with fresh ice water, and soak the sweetbreads for another 4 hours. Transfer to a colander and drain.

To prepare the foie gras, soak the blade of a thin, sharp knife in warm water, and wipe dry. With the warm blade, carefully slice the foie gras into 4 equal slices. Using a piece of waxed paper as a covering, gently press each slice with the palms of your hands, to create a nicely uniform piece with a searable, flat surface. Foie gras is totally pliable and forgiving; you can press together any miss-cut pieces and make any shapes you need. Lay the slices flat on a plate. With a very sharp, warmed knife, lightly score the foie's

I had grown restless in New York. I had made an agreement with myself that I would move on when I had learned what I needed to create the restaurant I wanted elsewhere. I decided to move to Sedona, Arizona, which struck me as very alluring and beautiful. Heading west, I stopped in Albuquerque for the night, unhitched my Jeep and drove to Santa Fe, straight to what I had come to think of as, "my building," which now housed a restaurant called The Carriage Trade.

I was disappointed; it looked terrible! Having dinner there, I realized the present owners hadn't understood the possibilities inherent in the building. The restaurant they had created wasn't a good fit—they had a popcorn machine in the middle of the front room!

After dinner, I returned to Albuquerque. Next morning, re-hitching the Jeep to the back of the truck, I told my partner, "I think we are making a terrible mistake. Why are we moving to Sedona when we should be moving to Santa Fe?"

Sedona was fun for a while, hiking, going to the Grand Canyon, fishing—it was truly beautiful. Interestingly, I kept meeting people from Santa Fe, who would say, "Why are you living in Sedona? You should move to Santa Fe."

It was inevitable. Santa Fe is a city that sends out a siren's call; the pull is irresistible.

In Santa Fe at last, I, of course, wound up living just up the street from "my building," now incarnated as The Borrego House.

Every day I would peek in the windows, until finally, I walked in and introduced myself to the owner, a magnificent older woman named Patricia Belvin. She was fascinating; I adored her. Each morning I'd stop by and we'd have coffee together.

The Borrego House restaurant was struggling. They too hadn't understood the potential of the building. The walls were orange, with lots of black wrought iron décor. It was quite a picture: orange dinner plates, green velvet bow ties and little dinner jackets on the waiters. It took me about six months to convince Patricia that she needed to sell me the restaurant. She never really belonged in the business; she was doing this to help out a friend. There she was, this beautiful matriarch, snow-white hair, impeccably dressed in Chanel suits—her father had been the Secretary of the Treasury under Roosevelt—she herself had a background in investment banking. She was perfect and precious and regal.

Cliff on . . . Getting It!

I would take Patricia huge bouquets of cymbidium orchids and Asian lilies. Talking and laughing together over demitasses of fine espresso, I'd ask here, "What the hell are you doing in this business?" She'd give me that Jackie O. smile, and inquire about the weather, or offer a compliment on my tie. I fell absolutely in love with her.

Finally, Patricia agreed to sell the restaurant to me. Somehow, mysteriously, I had known I would ultimately own this building. It had taken me fifteen years, and now that dream was becoming a reality.

Grilled Lobster Tails with Homemade Angel Hair Pasta and Spicy Chili Mayonnaise

Serves 4

Who would have thought that this simple dish would have such an impact? We have had literally thousands of requests for this recipe. Nearly every time a magazine calls for a story, they want the recipe for that "spicy lobster appetizer" that a reader has inquired about. Our faithful customers are also obsessed with this lobster dish. For all you lobster appetizer lovers, here it is! The pasta dough will need to rest for 1 hour before you make the angel hair, and you will need a pasta machine.

CHILI MAYONNAISE

1/4 cup red wine vinegar

1/4 cup freshly squeezed lemon juice

2 tablespoons light olive oil

2 tablespoons Dijon mustard

1 tablespoon minced garlic

2 tablespoons ground chili paste (sambal)

1/2 teaspoon finely minced seeded habanero pepper

2 cups aïoli (page 202)

Pinch of kosher salt

1 recipe pasta dough (page 210), or 1 pound angel hair pasta (if using dry pasta)

4 cold-water lobster tails, 4 to 6 ounces each

2 tablespoons light olive oil

Kosher salt

Freshly ground white pepper

2 tablespoons very finely diced chives, for garnish

To prepare the chili mayonnaise, combine the vinegar, lemon juice, olive oil, mustard, garlic, chili paste, habanero, aïoli, and salt in a nonreactive bowl. Whisk until all the ingredients are incorporated. Cover and refrigerate. This sauce can be prepared up to 1 week ahead and stored, covered tightly, in the refrigerator.

Prepare the pasta dough, and let it rest for at least an hour. Line a baking pan with parchment paper.

Roll out the dough to the thinnest setting on your pasta machine, then run the sheets of dough through the angel hair cutter attachment. This attachment is sometimes hard to come by; if need be, just use the finest setting; even the spaghetti-size cutter will work.

The pasta strands should be approximately 7 inches in length. As they come out, dust them with flour, and gently form them into small nests. Place the pasta nests in the baking pan.

To prepare the lobster for grilling, insert the tip of a very sharp French knife into the back of the lobster tail, right at the base, and cut straight down to slice the tail in half lengthwise. Turn the tail around, and cut the tailpiece in half. This will leave you with 2 pieces; do not remove the outer shell. Repeat the process for all 4 tails. Under cold water, rinse the tails and remove any veins that remain. Dry the tails with a paper towel. Place in a large bowl, cover with plastic wrap, and refrigerate until ready to grill.

Prepare a medium-hot fire in a charcoal grill, or preheat a gas grill to medium-high.

Place a large pot of salted water over high heat and bring to a boil.

Plunge the fresh angel hair pasta into the boiling water for about 1 minute, or until al dente. If you are using dry pasta, follow the directions on the package. Immediately transfer the pasta to a colander and drain. Transfer to a bowl and add half of the spicy mayonnaise. Toss very gently.

Remove the lobsters from the refrigerator and brush the meat side with the olive oil, salt, and white pepper. Place the lobsters, meat side down, on the grill, and cook for 3 minutes, until the edges of the shells begin to redden. Turn them over, and grill the shell side for 2 to 3 minutes, until the flesh is no longer translucent. Do not turn the lobster halves again, because valuable juices will be lost. The shell acts as a cup that holds some of the cooking liquid.

Warm 4 dinner plates.

Using a long-tined fork, swirl the pasta into 4 little nests, and set 1 on each plate. Arrange 2 pieces of the lobster on top of each nest. You can remove the shells if you wish: we leave them on for presentation and to preserve the juices that form in the shell.

Dollop the remaining mayonnaise around the lobster tails. Sprinkle the chives over the lobsters, and serve immediately.

Maryland Blue Crab Cakes with Caviar Sauce and Braised Leeks

Serves 4

There are a lot of notable crabmeats to use: Dungeness, Peekytoe, and even Jonah, but our favorite is the sweet Maryland blue crab. In the days of my youth, the annual summer vacation was always a trip to Rehoboth Beach, Maryland. We would go to a place called The Crab Pot where they cover the tables with thick brown packing paper and, literally, dump twenty or thirty steaming hot blue crabs, crusted with Old Bay seasoning, right on the paper with a big bottle of malt vinegar, bowls of melted butter, a bucket of steamed corn on the cob, and a roll of paper towels! Digging for the sweet fresh crabmeat was bliss. This recipe uses that sweet meat, couples it with a buttery caviar sauce, and creates a wonderful appetizer.

CRAB CAKES

1 pound Maryland jumbo lump crabmeat

2 tablespoons unsalted butter

1 cup very finely diced red bell pepper

2 tablespoons minced red onion

1 teaspoon minced garlic

1 teaspoon minced shallot

$^1/_2$ cup dry white wine

2 tablespoons malt vinegar

$^1/_4$ cup heavy cream

1 teaspoon crustacean spice (page 206)

1 teaspoon Dijon mustard

2 egg yolks

1 tablespoon fine chiffonade of basil

1 cup fresh white bread crumbs

$^1/_2$ cup fresh mayonnaise (page 209)

BRAISED LEEKS

2 young, tender leeks

1 tablespoon unsalted butter

Pinch of salt

Pinch of freshly ground white pepper

1 cup blonde chicken stock (page 213)

CAVIAR SAUCE

1 cup white butter sauce (page 212)

$^1/_2$ teaspoon chopped fresh dill

2 tablespoons osetra, sevruga, or American sturgeon caviar

Light olive oil, for sautéing

BABY WATERCRESS SALAD

1 cup watercress leaves, washed and dried

1 tablespoon extra virgin olive oil

Freshly squeezed juice of $^1/_2$ lemon

Pinch of sugar

Pinch of fleur de sel

To prepare the crab cakes, begin by cleaning the crabmeat. We actually do this under a black light, because the shells luminesce white. Paying close attention, carefully remove the shell pieces without breaking up the crabmeat too much: it is important that the cakes have nice-sized chunks of crab.

Place a sauté pan over medium heat and add the butter. When the butter has melted, add the pepper, onion, garlic, and shallot. Sauté for about 2 minutes, until the onion is translucent. Add the white wine and malt vinegar. Cook for 3 minutes, until the liquid is reduced by half. Add the heavy cream and cook for 3 minutes more, until reduced by half again. Add the crustacean spice, mayonnaise, and mustard and cook for 2 minutes, until the mixture begins to thicken.

Remove from the heat and cool for 5 minutes. Transfer to a bowl. Add the egg yolks and whisk well. Place the bowl over a larger bowl filled with ice water and chill for 30 minutes.

Transfer the chilled cream mixture to a large mixing bowl and add the crabmeat, basil, and bread crumbs. With a wooden spoon or rubber spatula, fold together very gently, as if you were making a very airy mousse.

Using a 2-inch ring mold, or just by hand, form the mixture into 8 nicely shaped cakes. Transfer to a large plate, cover, and refrigerate until ready to sauté.

To prepare the leeks, trim the leeks, reserving the green part for stock. Leeks are notoriously embedded with dirt, so soaking them in water and trimming them carefully is very important. Gently peel off any tough outer layers. Cut the white parts of the leeks into $1/4$-inch slices and soak in water again, making sure they are thoroughly clean. Drain in a small colander. Place a sauté pan over medium-low heat and add the butter. When the butter has melted, sauté the leek circles. Add the salt and white pepper. Add the chicken stock and simmer for about

3 minutes, or until the leek circles start to soften. Remove from the heat and set the leeks and stock in a warm place.

To prepare the caviar sauce, combine the butter sauce, dill, and caviar in a small ceramic bowl and set aside in a warm place.

Preheat the oven to 200°F. Prepare an ovenproof plate with several layers of paper towels.

To sauté the crab cakes, place a large, nonstick sauté pan over medium heat, and pour in a thin layer of olive oil. When the oil is hot, sauté the crab cakes, turning once, for 2 minutes per side, until golden brown. Transfer to the paper towels and drain. Remove the paper towels and place the plate of crab cakes in the oven.

To prepare the salad, place the watercress in a small bowl. In a separate small bowl, whisk together the olive oil, lemon juice, sugar, and salt. Pour over the watercress and toss gently to cover.

Set out 4 salad plates.

Transfer the leeks to a colander and drain. Using a slotted spoon, place a small mound of leek circles on each plate. Arrange 2 crab cakes on each, and spoon the sauce beside them. Mound a quarter of the watercress salad between the cakes, and serve immediately.

Scallop Mousse with Basil Lemon Espuma

Fish mousse is one of the amazing dishes I first experienced as an apprentice chef dining in New York's French restaurants. When we would go on these jaunts, a group of six, wide-eyed apprentices in our J. C. Penny polyester suits, not one of us older than twenty, with a seventy dollar expense account for two nights of dining, each of us earning about three cents an hour, we weren't exactly set up to eat a ten course meal at Lutèce. In spite of these extenuating circumstances, we were still intent on having a good time. The party boys would go off to party, while my friend, Jack Dile, and I, would go on eating adventures. He had a credit card, so we went first to Chinatown, then Little Italy, and, then, my first trip to the 21 Club. Though they weren't overly happy to see the likes of us, we did get a table. It was there that I had my first taste of a delicious pike mousse with a rich sauce vin blanc, accompanied by little peeled tomato diamonds, tiny parisenne zucchini balls and a large Coke! The arrival of that meal was one of those Moments, when I knew that the making of great food was what I wanted to do. I loved that mousse!

To prepare the mousse, you will need a gas-charged whipped cream dispenser, a thermometer, and six 4-ounce ramekins.

BASIL LEMON ESPUMA

3¼ cups water

2 cups basil leaves

6 sheets gelatin

¼ cup freshly squeezed lemon juice

1 tablespoon superfine sugar

SCALLOP MOUSSE

1 pound fresh sea scallops (connective muscle removed)

2 tablespoons minced shallot

1 cup heavy cream

2 egg yolks

1 egg

¼ cup dry white wine

20 leaves fresh tarragon

½ teaspoon sea salt

¼ teaspoon cayenne pepper

6 sprigs tarragon, for garnish

Zest of 1 lemon cut into strips, for garnish

Pour the water into a saucepan and bring to a boil over medium-high heat. Fill a bowl with ice water. Blanch the basil leaves in the boiling water for 15 seconds. Remove the leaves with a strainer. Reserve the blanching water. Plunge the leaves into the ice water bath and shock for about 1 minute, until thoroughly chilled. Immediately transfer the basil to a colander and drain, pressing out all the water. Transfer to a blender and purée until smooth. Press through a fine-mesh sieve into a small bowl.

Place the gelatin sheets, one at a time, into a large bowl. Cover with cold water and soak for 10 minutes, until soft.

Using a kitchen thermometer, check that your blanching water has cooled to around 140°F, and then add the gelatin sheets to it, one at a time. Mix in the lemon juice, sugar, and basil purée and cool to room temperature. Whisk the espuma until smooth, pour it into a whipped cream dispenser, and refrigerate.

Preheat the oven to 300°F. Butter 6 (4-ounce) ramekins.

To prepare the mousse, place the scallops in a food processor and purée until smooth. Slowly add the shallot, cream, egg yolks, whole egg, white wine, and tarragon leaves. Process until blended and smooth. Add the salt and cayenne pepper and process for another 30 seconds.

Transfer to a bowl. Place over a larger bowl filled with ice water and keep chilled. When making mousses that need to be cooked, it is important to keep them well chilled prior to cooking.

Divide the mousse equally among the ramekins and set them in a shallow baking pan. Fill the pan with water halfway up the sides of the ramekins.

Cover the pan with a layer of plastic wrap and a layer of aluminum foil. Place in the oven for 40 to 50 minutes, until a skewer inserted gently in the center comes out clean and the mousse feels firm but still spongy.

Gently invert each mousse onto a flat plate, being careful not to break them. Set out 6 small plates. Use the whipped cream dispenser to foam out a 4-inch pool of the espuma on each plate. With a spatula, gently set a warm mousse in the center of the espuma on each plate. Garnish each with a tarragon sprig and some of the lemon zest. Serve immediately.

Ahi Tuna, Smoked Salmon, and Avocado Tartare with Snap Pea and Gari Salad and Chive Buttermilk Pancakes

Serves 4

Many tartare lovers crave the original chopped beef version made with capers, parsley, onions, mustard, and egg yolk and served with a crunchy crostini. This tartare, made with tuna, is every bit as luscious—both light and rich, with an Asian flair.

The pillowy pancakes beautifully set off this coupling of the fresh fish mélange with silky smooth avocado.

CHIVE BUTTERMILK PANCAKES

3/4 cup all-purpose flour

1/2 teaspoon baking powder

2 tablespoons minced chives

1/2 teaspoon sugar

Pinch of salt

1/4 cup buttermilk

1 egg

1 egg yolk

1/2 teaspoon toasted sesame oil

TUNA, SMOKED SALMON, AND AVOCADO TARTARE

8 ounces very fresh ahi tuna, finely diced

4 ounces smoked salmon, finely diced

1 teaspoon very finely diced red onion

1 teaspoon sesame seeds, toasted, and cooled (page 219)

1 tablespoon toasted sesame oil

3 very fresh quail egg yolks, or 1 very fresh chicken egg yolk

1 teaspoon mustard vinaigrette (page 210)

1 teaspoon small capers

2 pinches of fleur de sel

1 pinch of freshly ground white pepper

1/2 cup very ripe, finely diced avocado

SNAP PEA AND GARI SALAD

4 cups water

1 teaspoon kosher salt

1/2 cup julienned snap peas

1/2 cup tender frisée (the yellow white center part)

1/4 cup julienned gari (Japanese pickled ginger)

1 teaspoon finely diced green onion

Freshly squeezed juice of 1 lemon

1 tablespoon extra virgin olive oil

1 tablespoon honey

Pinch of fleur de sel

Fresh wasabi cream (page 207), for garnish

To prepare the pancake batter, in a mixing bowl, combine the flour, baking powder, chives, sugar, and salt and whisk together. In a separate small bowl, whisk together the buttermilk, egg, egg yolk, and sesame oil. Make a well in the center of the flour mixture, and pour in the wet ingredients. Whisk together for about 30 seconds, or just until incorporated. The tendency is to mix until there are absolutely no lumps, and for some things that is fine, but not for a light and fluffy pancake.

To prepare the tartare, in a mixing bowl, combine the tuna, salmon, onion, sesame seeds, sesame oil, egg yolks, mustard vinaigrette, capers, salt, and white pepper and mix lightly with a small wooden spoon. Take care not to mash or overmix the ingredients; just gently commingle and coat each item with the dressing, to preserve the succulence of each of the components. After mixing thoroughly, gently fold in the avocado.

To blanch the peas, pour the water into a saucepan and add the salt. Bring to a boil over high heat. Fill a bowl with ice water. Blanch the peas in the boiling water for about 2 minutes. Using a slotted spoon or strainer, transfer the peas to the ice water bath. Shock for about 1 minute, or until thoroughly chilled. Immediately transfer the peas to a colander and drain.

To prepare the salad, in a mixing bowl, toss together the frisée, peas, gari, and green onion. In another small bowl, whisk together the lemon juice, olive oil, honey, and salt. Pour over the salad and gently toss. Cover and refrigerate until ready to serve.

Heat a griddle over medium heat and coat with canola oil.

With a small spoon or ladle, drop 2-inch dollops of pancake batter on the griddle. Cook for about

1 minute, until the pancakes start to bubble and look golden brown on the underside. With a thin spatula, flip them over, and cook just until done, 30 to 45 seconds. Remove from the griddle and keep warm and covered with a slightly damp towel. This makes about 16 little cakes.

To assemble, equally divide the tartare among 4 of your favorite Asian-style white plates, shaping it neatly using a ring mold or just forming a nice quenelle or small oval shape. Gently retoss the salad, and form the greens into mounds next to the tartare. Fan out 4 of the pancakes alongside the salad. With a tiny spoon or squirt bottle, place little droplets of the wasabi cream around the plate. Serve immediately.

On Friday, November 30, 1990, no one at what was then The Borrego House knew I had actually bought the restaurant. It had been a very quiet transaction.

That morning, at about eight o'clock, using the keys to the building, I came in with a little cash drawer that fit into the register. I walked around, introducing myself to the bewildered staff, shaking hands and saying, "Hello, my name is Cliff Skoglund, and I'm the new owner of this restaurant. I want to let you know that everything's fine, and I need your help to do this. Please continue doing whatever it is that you do."

Cliff on . . . Starting Up

I went back into the kitchen and talked to the cooks, assuring them that they should just do what they always did, and asking if they needed anything.

Then we opened for lunch!

In the kitchen was a tiny grill, only half of which worked. The chef was smoking a cigarette, while flipping these mysterious little things, which turned out on closer inspection to be chicken tenders. And they were making duck burritos: thawed duck meat rolled in a tortilla, and thrown in the microwave. Sending them out, for eighteen, nineteen dollars.

I knew that the vision I had would be in place very soon; at that moment, the most important thing was to serve lunch. I was there all day, then we closed, cleaned up, and reopened for dinner. The house regulars began to arrive. I stood at the door, smiling, saying, "Hi, how are you?" And inquisitively, they would return, "Hi, uhn, who are you?"

Afterwards I stayed there most of the night, trying to figure out the keys, doors, and alarms, all of it. I went home, slept for an hour or two, came back Saturday morning, and did the same thing, and came back in on Sunday through brunch and dinner.

By Sunday night, I was dead tired. I crawled into bed in my little adobe house that I had thought was going to be so cute. It was ancient; if you know anything about old adobes, you know the roofs are insulated with earth.

I pulled the covers up to my neck, and a huge clod of dirt fell through a crack in the ceiling and smacked me on the forehead. Suddenly the realization of it all hit me. What was I thinking? What had I done?

I had done something terrific, I reminded myself—I had begun the process of building Geronimo.

Crispy Skate on Rocket Salad with Lime and Shrimp Vinaigrette

Serves 4

Skate does not get the recognition it deserves. I love the tenderness and natural butteriness of this flavorful fish. In this dish, the contrasting textures are great, and the tangy vinaigrette complements the richness of the fish. Skate, known to the French as raie, is a seasonal fish, and very perishable. Don't let this stop you, because skate is a treat you should not miss. So be sure to consult your local fishmonger about availability and freshness.

The shrimp we use in our vinaigrette are tiny bay shrimp. Butch, our fish purveyor from Above Sea Level (see page 200), found a great source for nice fresh ones; they are so sweet and tender. If you can't find bay shrimp, a good quality-salad shrimp is an excellent substitute.

LIME AND SHRIMP VINAIGRETTE

8 ounces shelled bay shrimp

$1/4$ cup freshly squeezed lime juice

1 teaspoon crustacean spice (page 206)

1 teaspoon Dijon mustard

1 teaspoon minced shallot

1 tablespoon honey

$1/3$ cup extra virgin olive oil

$1/2$ teaspoon chopped fresh dill

Fleur de sel

Freshly cracked white pepper

$1/2$ cup glutinous rice flour

$1/2$ cup mung bean flour

Sea salt

Freshly ground white pepper

4 pieces of fresh skate fillet, 6 to 8 ounces each

2 tablespoons unsalted butter

3 tablespoons peanut oil

1 pound rocket (arugula), cleaned and dried

To prepare the vinaigrette, place a pot of salted water over medium-high heat and bring to a boil. Add the shrimp and cook for about 1 minute, until pink and just cooked through. Remove from the heat and transfer to a colander to drain. Transfer the shrimp to a bowl set over a larger bowl filled with ice water, and keep cold.

In a stainless steel or glass bowl, combine the lime juice, crustacean spice, mustard, shallot, and honey. Whisk vigorously until well blended. Slowly drizzle the olive oil into the mixture, whisking continuously until it is incorporated. Fold in the dill and shrimp. Season to taste with fleur de sel and cracked white pepper. If you're going to prepare the fish immediately, set this vinaigrette aside at room temperature; if not, cover and refrigerate until ready to serve. This dressing will need to be whisked right before serving, because the oil will separate from the other ingredients.

To prepare the skate, in a shallow pan or pie plate, stir the rice flour and mung bean flour together with a fork until fully blended.

Salt and pepper the skate fillets on both sides and dredge them in the flour mixture until they are thoroughly coated. Sometimes a gentle redredging is necessary to completely coat the fish.

Set out a plate with several layers of paper towels.

Place a sauté pan over medium-high heat and add the butter. When the butter is brown, add the peanut oil. When the oil is hot, place the skate in

the pan, rounded side down. Cook each side for 4 to
5 minutes, until the flesh is crispy. Transfer to the
paper towels to drain. Keep warm.

To assemble, gently toss half of the vinaigrette
with the rocket and evenly divide the salad among
4 large plates. Set a warm fillet atop each salad.
Ladle some of the remaining vinaigrette over the
fish and around the plate, showcasing the shrimp.
Serve immediately.

Morel Mushroom Tarts with Foie Gras and Black Truffle

Serves 6

This recipe is a homage to one of the greatest chefs ever, Joël Robuchon. Without his books, and his willingness to share his philosophy, growing up in this business would not have been as passionate and pleasurable. These tarts are a decadent and wonderful surprise for your guests, who will savor every bite. This recipe does require that you begin at least a day or two in advance. You will need cheesecloth and six 3-inch fluted tart pans with removable bottoms.

FOIE GRAS

1 whole foie gras, about 1^1/$_2$ pounds, cleaned and deveined

8 cups milk

^{1}/$_4$ teaspoon kosher salt

^{1}/$_8$ teaspoon pink salt

2 shallots, minced

1 black truffle, very finely diced

^{1}/$_2$ cup Cognac

8 cups blonde chicken stock (page 213)

TART SHELLS

2^1/$_2$ cups all-purpose flour

^{1}/$_2$ teaspoon salt

^{1}/$_4$ teaspoon baking powder

1 cup cold, unsalted butter, cut into 1-inch cubes

6 tablespoons ice water

FILLING

2 tablespoons unsalted butter

1^1/$_2$ pounds cleaned and stemmed morel mushrooms, about 2 cups

1 teaspoon minced fresh garlic

2 tablespoons minced shallot

Kosher salt

Freshly ground black pepper

^{1}/$_2$ cup dry white wine

1 cup brown chicken stock (page 214)

SALAD

^{1}/$_2$ cup mâche

1 cup frisée

^{1}/$_2$ cup julienned red onion

1 tablespoon white truffle oil

1 tablespoon extra virgin olive oil

1^1/$_2$ teaspoons cider vinegar

Pinch of salt

High-quality extra virgin olive oil, for drizzling

To prepare the foie gras, place the foie gras in a large bowl and add the milk. Cover and refrigerate overnight to draw out some of the residual blood.

Set out a plate with several layers of paper towels.

Remove the foie from the refrigerator. Transfer to a colander and rinse under cold running water. Transfer to the paper towels and dry thoroughly. Remove any outer skin on the liver. Slice horizontally three-quarters of the way through the pieces, and fan them open. Place the foie in a ceramic bowl and sprinkle with the salt, pink salt, shallot, and black truffle. Stir together gently with a folding motion, taking care not to break up the pieces of foie. Sprinkle the Cognac over all the pieces. Cover and refrigerate for 3 hours. Remove from the refrigerator, and let set at room temperature for 1 hour.

After the pieces of foie gras soften a bit, separate the liver into 3 equal parts. Place each piece on a 12 by 12-inch sheet of parchment paper. Roll each

piece, shaping the liver into 3 tubes about 1 inch in diameter and about 12 inches in length.

Rinse a piece of cheesecloth to remove any cloth particles. Remove the parchment paper from the liver tubes and reroll them in the cheesecloth. Make sure to roll the ends tightly to help hold the shape of the foie gras, and secure the ends with a string. Place the tubes in a baking pan. Cover and refrigerate.

Fill a large bowl with ice water.

Place a shallow, 12-inch-long flameproof baking pan over medium-low heat. Fill it with the chicken stock, and bring it to a simmer. Remove the tubes from the refrigerator and place all 3 into the simmering stock for about 1 minute. Remove the tubes and shock them in the ice water bath for 1 minute, until thoroughly chilled. Transfer to a clean, dry baking pan. Cover and refrigerate overnight.

To prepare the tart shells, combine the flour, salt, and baking powder in a food processor. Pulse for 2 seconds, until blended. Add the cold butter cubes, and pulse about 15 times, or until the mixture resembles coarsely ground cornmeal. Sprinkle the ice water on top. Pulse for about 10 seconds, until the dough just holds together; do not overmix. Transfer to a lightly floured surface and form a smooth ball of dough, being careful not to work it too much, as that will make it tough. Wrap the dough in plastic wrap and refrigerate for 20 minutes. Butter 6 (3-inch) fluted removable-bottom tart pans.

Remove the dough from the refrigerator and place on a floured surface. Divide the dough into 6 equal balls, handling it as little as possible. Work with 1 portion of dough at a time, reserving the others, wrapped, in the refrigerator.

Preheat the oven to 350°F.

On a lightly floured surface, roll out the ball of dough into a circle 7 inches in diameter and $1/8$ inch thick. Gently fold the circle in half, then in half again, so you can lift it without tearing. Place the point of the folded dough in the center of a buttered tart pan, carefully unfold the circle, and tenderly press the dough into the tart pan. Trim the edges by running a rolling pin over the top. Score the bottom of the tart shell 3 times with a fork, and refrigerate until ready to bake. Repeat this process for all.

Place the shells in the oven and bake for 15 minutes, or until golden brown. Remove from the oven and let cool at room temperature.

To prepare the filling, place a sauté pan over medium heat, and melt the butter. Add the mushrooms, garlic, shallot, salt, and pepper, and sauté for 2 minutes, until soft. Add the white wine and chicken stock and cook for about 5 minutes, until all the liquid is absorbed. Set in a warm place.

To assemble, remove the tart shells from the pans and set each on a small plate. Divide the mushroom mixture equally among the tart shells. Spread the mushrooms evenly. Remove the foie gras tubes from the refrigerator and place on a cutting surface. Carefully unwrap the cheesecloth. Using a warm knife dipped in hot water and dried, cut the foie gras into $1/4$-inch slices, creating little disks. There should be approximately 60 disks. Arrange the disks in a circle around the inside edges of the tarts.

To prepare the salad, combine the mâche, frisée, and red onion in a bowl. Sprinkle with the truffle oil, olive oil, vinegar, and salt. Toss gently. Set a little mound of salad in the center of each tart. Drizzle with a really special extra virgin olive oil, and serve.

Egg Griddled Goat Cheese and Smoked Salmon with Chicory Salad and Crispy Lardons

Serves 6

Wonderful goat cheese is made in many different places, and many superb ones come from New Mexico. My very favorite is from Sweetwoods Dairy, (see page 199). We take this fantastic cheese, add a small amount of smoked salmon and some minced green onion, coat it with an egg batter, and griddle-fry it in butter. This dish is a real treat if you love salad and cheese, as I do.

8 ounces slab bacon

1 pound fresh goat cheese, about 1¹/₂ cups

8 ounces smoked salmon, diced

¹/₄ cup minced green onion

1 teaspoon minced capers

¹/₂ teaspoon freshly ground black pepper

¹/₂ cup all-purpose flour

CHICORY SALAD

8 cups chicory (frisée), washed and dried

Pinch of kosher salt

¹/₄ cup basic vinaigrette (page 203)

4 eggs

¹/₂ cup panko crumbs

¹/₄ cup canola oil

Prepare a dinner plate with several layers of paper towels.

To prepare the lardons, cut the slab bacon into small batonnets, ¹/₈ inch wide by ¹/₂ inch long. Heat a nonstick sauté pan over medium heat. When the pan is hot, add the lardons, and stir. Separate them as the fat renders. Cook for 8 to 10 minutes, until they are brown and crisp. Be careful not to overcook; remember that there will be some residual cooking after they are removed from the fat. Remove the lardons from the pan with a slotted spoon, transfer to the paper towels, and drain.

To prepare the goat cheese rounds, in a bowl, beat the goat cheese with a wooden spoon until fairly smooth. Fold in the smoked salmon, green onion, capers, and pepper.

Line a baking pan with a layer of plastic wrap.

Divide the cheese into 6 equal portions and roll as you would a meatball. Place the flour in a small bowl and dredge the balls in the flour, coating them thoroughly. Place the balls about 3 inches apart in the baking pan. Lay another sheet of plastic wrap on top of the cheese balls. Gently press down with a flat spatula to form a 1-inch-thick patty. Place the pan in the freezer for 10 minutes.

Chill 6 salad plates.

To prepare the salad, in a bowl, combine the chicory, lardons, and salt. Add the vinaigrette and toss gently. Divide into even mounds on the salad plates.

To sauté the cheese rounds, in a small bowl, whisk the eggs until fluffy. Add the panko crumbs and whisk thoroughly.

Prepare a plate with several layers of paper towels.

Place a nonstick sauté pan over medium heat and add the oil. Remove the cheese rounds from the freezer. Dip each one into the egg batter, coating well. When the oil is hot, fry the cheese rounds, 2 at a time, turning once, for about 1 minute per side, until golden brown. Transfer to the paper towels and drain. Place a cheese round on each plate, beside the salad. Serve immediately.

Entrées

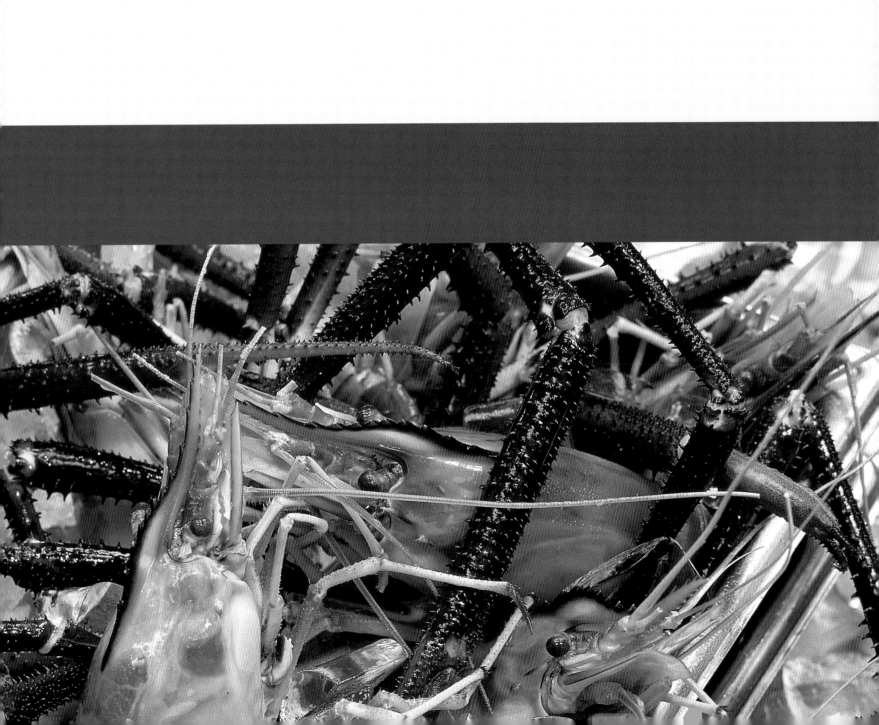

Mesquite-Grilled Peppery Elk Tenderloin with Garlic Confit Potatoes and Exotic Mushroom Sauce

Serves 4

This is a signature dish for us, actually a destination item on our menu, year round. Many dining enthusiasts come to Geronimo specifically for this dish, and we receive literally hundreds of requests for the recipe. Basically, this is an extravagant, luscious version of meat-and-potatoes comfort food. The elk is ruby red in color, rich in flavor, buttery, and fork-tender. And the potatoes—garlicky, fork-mashed, they are soothing and hearty, an utterly pleasurable, down-home epicurean feast.

MARINADE

1 bottle (12 ounces) dark Mexican beer, such as Negra Modelo or Dos Equis Dark

3 cloves garlic, minced

1 tablespoon very finely diced shallot

$1/4$ cup hoisin sauce

$1/4$ cup light soy sauce

2 sprigs rosemary

4 trimmed pieces of elk tenderloin, 8 ounces each

MUSHROOM SAUCE

2 tablespoons unsalted butter

8 ounces fresh morels, soaked in several changes of warm water and rinsed thoroughly, about 1 cup

8 ounces trimmed and halved chanterelles, washed and gently brushed clean, about 1 cup

8 ounces stemmed and sliced criminis, washed and gently brushed clean, about 1 cup

3 shallots, minced

1 teaspoon kosher salt

1 teaspoon freshly ground black pepper

1 cup dry white wine

1 cup veal demi-glace (page 212)

1 cup blonde chicken stock (page 213)

$1/4$ cup heavy cream

1 tablespoon fresh thyme leaves

GARLIC CONFIT POTATOES

2 pounds medium Yukon Gold potatoes

2 slices applewood-smoked bacon

$1/4$ cup unsalted butter

$1/4$ cup mashed garlic confit (page 208)

$1^1/2$ teaspoons kosher salt

$1/2$ teaspoon freshly cracked white pepper

1 cup half-and-half

2 tablespoons finely minced fresh chives

1 tablespoon kosher salt

2 tablespoons freshly ground black pepper

$1/4$ cup raw peanut oil

To prepare the marinade, combine the beer, garlic, shallot, hoisin sauce, soy sauce, and rosemary in a small bowl and whisk together.

Arrange the tenderloins in a glass or ceramic bowl. Thoroughly coat the meat with the marinade. Cover and refrigerate for at least 12 hours.

To prepare the mushroom sauce, place a saucepan over medium-high heat and add the butter. When the butter has melted, add the morels, chanterelles, criminis, shallot, salt, and pepper, and sauté, stirring frequently, for 4 to 5 minutes, until they begin to brown. Deglaze the pan with the white wine and cook for 4 minutes, until most of the liquid has evaporated. Add the veal demi-glace, chicken stock, heavy cream, and thyme. Decrease the heat to low. Simmer for 10 minutes, until the sauce starts to thicken. The sauce should become the consistency of a thick mushroom stew or ragout. Remove from the heat. Cover and set in a warm place.

Prepare a plate with several layers of paper towels.

To prepare the potatoes, bring a large pot of salted water to a boil over high heat. Boil the unpeeled potatoes for about 20 minutes, until fork-tender. Remove from the heat and transfer the potatoes to a colander, draining off the water. Set over a bowl in a warm place. Place a small sauté pan over medium heat, add the bacon, and fry until cooked through but not crispy. Remove from the heat, and transfer the bacon to the paper towels. Drain well and mince with a sharp knife. Cut the cooked potatoes into 1/2-inch cubes.

Place large sauté pan over medium heat and add 2 tablespoons of the butter. When the butter starts to brown, add the potatoes, garlic confit, bacon, salt, and cracked white pepper. Fold together with a wooden spoon. Add the half-and-half, stir again, and decrease the heat to low. Slowly simmer the

potato mixture for about 10 minutes, until thick and bubbling. Coarsely mash with a large-tined fork or potato masher. Add the remaining 2 tablespoons of butter and the chives. Stir, adding more salt if desired. Cover and set in a warm place.

Prepare a medium-hot fire in a mesquite charcoal grill, or preheat a gas grill to medium-high.

Remove the elk from the marinade and pat dry. Rub with salt and pepper—be sure to use all the pepper. Drizzle the oil over the meat and turn to coat thoroughly. Grill evenly, turning frequently, for 3 to 4 minutes per side, or until the meat is the desired doneness. Since elk has very little fat, we grill ours to medium rare for best flavor and nice, juicy texture.

Place the saucepan with the mushroom sauce over low heat and heat for 3 to 4 minutes, until gently simmering.

Place a generous scoop of mashed potatoes in the center of each dinner plate. Ladle the mushroom sauce over the potatoes. Place the peppery elk tenderloins on the mound of potatoes, and serve immediately.

We all know that a particular smell can stir up deep and powerful memories of people, situations, places from the past, and, most of all for me, food memories.

And not just memories of eating at different places, but the scene, the stage, the performances, the comedy acts of the kitchen.

For instance, when I smell bacon cooking I immediately think of a veteran breakfast guru, the first line cook I ever worked with, who went by the illustrious name of Hooty.

Hooty would come in at the ungodly hour of 3 A.M. and begin cooking bacon for breakfast parties, buffets, and the staff—literally a ton of bacon. He was fabulous at his job, and he was mean. Besides grunting out orders at me as a first-year apprentice slave, it took him two weeks to learn my name and realize I was there for the long haul.

I'll never forget the 6:59 A.M. procession of waiters coming down the ramp to the kitchen, yelling out egg orders: "threeovermediumwithsausage," "twokipperswithsunny-sides," "oneGruyèreomelettewithbacon."

Mean old Hooty was in control: he could handle about eight egg pans, cooking each order to perfection, and still have enough time to demoralize every waiter that entered the kitchen.

I was in awe.

So, during my tenure at the breakfast station, I would also arrive at that ungodly hour, just to see how this toque-rejecting artist—he refused to wear a chef's hat, only an old white skullcap and a dishwasher's shirt—mastered this high-wire performance. Working with him, I knew why he was the only one in the kitchen who could break dress code. He was the Michael Jordan of the breakfast line.

Eric's Memory Lane

Grilled Veal Porterhouse Steaks with Sweet Potato Flan and Prosciutto Caper Sauce

Serves 4

This hearty dish lends itself beautifully to being prepared a day or two in advance of serving. The flan can be cooked, refrigerated, and then cut out like cookies. The caper sauce, chilled, holds well overnight. Grilling the veal is the only step that needs to be done just before serving. We use a thick, voluptuously tender cut of veal for the steak lover. A porterhouse steak contains a greater percentage of the tenderloin than its brother, the T-bone, thus making it a great piece of meat.

This is a wonderful dish—deeply satisfying and loaded with flavor from the savory combination of prosciutto and capers. It's about coming to the table with a good appetite and getting fed on many levels: the milky flesh of the meat, the rich, rustic flan, and the tangy caper sauce.

SWEET POTATO FLAN

2 medium-large sweet potatoes (about 2 pounds)

2 medium-large Yukon Gold potatoes (about 1 pound)

1 tablespoon unsalted butter

1/2 cup diced yellow onion

1 tablespoon minced garlic

3 eggs

1 cup heavy cream

2 tablespoons chopped fresh Italian parsley

1/2 cup grated sharp cheddar cheese

1/2 cup grated Parmesan cheese

2 tablespoons kosher salt

1 tablespoon freshly, finely ground white pepper

4 quarts water

4 tablespoons kosher salt

16 jumbo asparagus spears, trimmed and peeled

PROSCIUTTO CAPER SAUCE

1 tablespoon unsalted butter

2 shallots, thinly sliced

2 cups dry vermouth

2 sprigs thyme

2 bay leaves

1 teaspoon freshly cracked black pepper

1 cup blonde chicken stock (page 213)

1 cup glace de viande (page 209)

1 cup half-and-half

2 tablespoons Creole mustard

1/4 cup nonpareil capers

1/4 cup diced prosciutto

2 tablespoons minced fresh tarragon

4 veal porterhouse steaks, 14 to 16 ounces each

Kosher salt

Freshly cracked black pepper

1/4 cup canola oil

2 tablespoons unsalted butter

Freshly ground white pepper

4 sprigs oregano and/or rosemary, for garnish

To prepare the flan, wash and peel the sweet potatoes and Yukon gold potatoes. Place them in a large bowl with enough cool water to cover, to keep them from discoloring.

Place a small sauté pan over medium-low heat and add the butter. When the butter has melted, add the onion and garlic, and sweat for about 3 minutes, until the onion is translucent. Remove from the heat.

In a mixing bowl, with a wire whisk, gently whip the eggs and heavy cream. Stir in the parsley,

sautéed onion and garlic, cheddar, Parmesan, salt, and white pepper until thoroughly incorporated. Cover and refrigerate.

Preheat the oven to 400°F.

Pat the potatoes dry and slice them paper-thin with a very sharp knife. Carefully place them into a large mixing bowl. Or slice the potatoes on a mandoline and let them fall into the mixing bowl. Once the potatoes are all sliced, gently mix them with your hands to mingle the two varieties. Pour the egg mixture over the potatoes, and mix very gently to coat the potatoes, taking care not to crumble the potato slices.

Oil a 12 by 12-inch glass or ceramic oven-safe baking dish.

Carefully spread the potatoes in the baking dish, and press down lightly. Scrape out the mixing bowl with a rubber spatula and pour any remaining egg mixture into the baking dish. Evenly smooth and flatten the top surface.

Place the baking dish in the center of the hot oven for 15 to 20 minutes, until the potato mixture begins to brown slightly. Decrease the oven temperature to 325°F. Cover the potatoes with a lid and continue baking for 45 to 55 minutes. Test for doneness by piercing the flan with a table knife; it should come out clean. Remove from the oven, let cool on a rack, and refrigerate until chilled.

To blanch the asparagus, pour the water into a large saucepan and add the salt. Bring to a boil over high heat. Fill a large bowl with ice water. Blanch the asparagus in the boiling water for 4 minutes, until al dente. Using a slotted spoon or strainer, transfer the asparagus to the ice water bath. Shock

for about 1 minute, or until thoroughly chilled. Immediately transfer the asparagus to a colander and drain. Transfer to a plate and cover.

To prepare the caper sauce, place a saucepan over medium-low heat and add the butter. When the butter has melted, add the shallots and sauté for about 2 minutes, until slightly brown. Add the dry vermouth, thyme, bay leaves, and cracked pepper. Decrease the heat to low and cook for 10 minutes, until the liquid is reduced by half. Remove and discard the bay leaves and thyme sprigs. Pour in the chicken stock, glace de viande, half-and-half, mustard, capers, and prosciutto. Increase the heat to medium-low and cook for 20 minutes, until slightly thickened, occasionally skimming the impurities off the surface and discarding. Stir in the tarragon, and remove from the heat.

Oil a baking pan.

Cut the chilled flan into circles with a 3-inch cookie cutter and place them in the baking pan.

To grill the veal, prepare a medium-hot fire in a charcoal grill, or preheat a gas grill to medium-high.

Preheat the oven to 400°F.

Season the veal with the salt and cracked pepper. Coat it well with the oil. As odd as it sounds, stand the steaks up, with the bone side down on the grill, for about 5 minutes. This cooks the meat closest to the bone.

Grill the veal to medium rare, about 5 minutes on each side.

During the final 5 minutes of grilling the veal, place the flan circles into the oven and bake for 4 to 5 minutes, until hot and slightly puffed. Rewarm the sauce over low heat.

To prepare the asparagus, place a sauté pan over medium-low heat and add the butter. When the butter has melted, add the asparagus spears, with salt and white pepper to taste. Sauté for 2 minutes, or just until hot. Remove from the heat, and keep warm.

Warm a large serving platter.

On the platter, stand the veal steaks, bone side down, in a row. Place the flan circles along one side of the steaks; arrange the asparagus over the flan.

Garnish with the herb sprigs. Serve the sauce on the side.

Tournedos of Beef with Spinach Potato Flan, Port Reduction Sauce, and Herb Garlic Compound Butter

Serves 4

Tournedos of beef are the pieces of tenderloin that are at the heart of the loin.

Basically, they are very lean and quite a bit smaller than the monster filet mignon that you may get at your favorite steak house. So, what's the big deal with tournedos? In every French-based kitchen I ever worked, tournedos were a prized and often-ordered dish. And, since they are normally served in pairs, they make a flashy presentation.

Tournedos also have a very illustrious culinary history. The indispensable culinary encyclopedia, Larousse Gastronomique, notes that the famous composer Rossini, yes, a fellow Italian, frequently requested tournedos with foie gras and truffle sauce in a noted Paris restaurant, an extravagance which so shocked the head waiter, that he had the dish served behind the backs, or "dans le dos," of the other customers.

I love serving these two petite steaks with a rich port reduction and a creamy potato flan.

You will need parchment paper and a mandoline for this recipe.

HERB GARLIC COMPOUND BUTTER

6 tablespoons unsalted butter, at room temperature

1 tablespoon fresh thyme leaves

1 tablespoon minced fresh chives

1 tablespoon minced garlic

$1/2$ teaspoon minced shallot

1 teaspoon kosher salt

$1/2$ teaspoon freshly ground black pepper

SPINACH POTATO FLAN

$2^1/2$ cups water

3 tablespoons kosher salt

1 cup chopped spinach

3 eggs

2 egg yolks

1 cup heavy cream

$1/4$ teaspoon freshly grated nutmeg

1 teaspoon salt

Pinch of freshly ground white pepper

1 cup shredded Asiago cheese

3 medium russet potatoes

PORT REDUCTION SAUCE

1 cup veal demi-glace (page 212)

1 cup port wine

8 tournedos of beef tenderloin, 4 ounces each

Kosher salt

Freshly ground black pepper

Light olive oil, for rubbing on tournedos

Sliced disks of red bell pepper, for garnish

Cut a 15 by 15-inch piece of parchment paper.

To prepare the butter, place the butter, thyme, chives, garlic, shallot, salt, and pepper in a small bowl. Using a wooden spoon, cream well. On the parchment paper, press the butter into a log shape, about 4 inches long, placing the butter log 3 inches in from the edge that is closest to you. Roll the parchment away from you, around the butter, until it forms a tube. Twist the ends of the tube, like a wrapped piece of saltwater taffy, tightening until the tube is hard and uniform in size. Refrigerate for at least 1 hour. Unwrap and cut the butter tube into $1/2$-inch disks.

To prepare the flan, pour the water into a saucepan and add the salt. Bring to a boil over medium-high heat. Fill a bowl with ice water. Blanch the spinach in the boiling water for 15 seconds. Using a slotted spoon or strainer, transfer the leaves to the ice water bath. Shock for about 1 minute, or until cold. Immediately transfer the spinach to a colander and drain. Press out all the water.

Preheat the oven to 400°F. Butter a 9 by 9-inch glass or ceramic baking dish.

In a large bowl, mix together the eggs, egg yolks, cream, nutmeg, salt, white pepper, spinach, and cheese until smooth.

Peel the potatoes, and slice very thin on a mandoline. Add the potatoes to the egg and cream mixture, and pour into the baking dish. Cover the baking dish with plastic wrap and a top layer of aluminum foil. Place in the center of the oven and bake for 50 minutes, or until a knife comes out clean.

To prepare the sauce, place a small saucepan over medium heat, add the port, and reduce by half.

Add the demi-glace and bring to a simmer. Remove from the heat. Strain through a fine chinois into a bowl.

To prepare the tournedos, tie a string around the circumference of the meat, to keep it uniform and prevent separation of the fibers. This also helps keep valuable moisture from escaping an already very lean piece of meat. Heat a cast iron, or heavy-bottomed skillet over high heat. Salt and pepper the tournedos and rub olive oil over them. Sear the steaks, turning once, for about 2 minutes per side, until nicely browned on each side. Transfer the tournedos to a plate, and remove the string. Set a disc of the garlic herb butter on each.

To serve, spoon out 2 (2-inch) mounds of the potatoes onto each of 4 dinner plates. Put 2 slices of the red pepper on the potatoes. Place a tournedo on each mound. Spoon the sauce around the potato flan and serve immediately.

Wasabi-Crusted Rack of Colorado Lamb with Ginger Mint Syrup and Fried Soba Noodle Cakes

Serves 6

What makes this dish so fun and delicious, besides the scrumptious Colorado lamb, is the flavor and kick of fresh wasabi. There is a huge difference between fresh and powdered wasabi. Powdered wasabi, which is relatively inexpensive, is actually horseradish and mustard powder, with food coloring added. Fresh wasabi has a distinctly clean, crisp taste that is not as sharply bitter as some imitation powders can be. We acquire ours from Pacific Farms, (see page 222) which at this time is the only commercial grower of this prized rhizomic vegetable in North America.

This recipe's distinct Asian flair complements the lamb quite well. Reduce the cooking time by about half if you are using a New Zealand lamb or a spring, baby lamb. We use a process of oven blanching for the lamb, which means the final cooking time is less, so as not to burn the wasabi crust.

---

2 racks excellent-quality lamb, 9 bones each, frenched and chine removed (page 218)

Kosher salt

Freshly ground black pepper

Canola oil, for rubbing on lamb

1/2 cup freshly grated wasabi paste

3 whole eggs

1 cup fresh bread crumbs

2 tablespoons garlic confit (page 208)

1/2 cup all-purpose flour

GINGER MINT SYRUP

3 tablespoons grated fresh ginger

1 tablespoon apple cider vinegar

1/2 cup honey

2 tablespoons chopped shallot

2 cups apple juice

Pinch of salt

8 whole black peppercorns

1 cup finely chopped fresh mint leaves

SOBA NOODLE CAKES

4 ounces soba noodles (4 cups cooked)

3 tablespoons light soy sauce

1 tablespoon cornstarch

3 eggs

1/2 cup chopped green onion

2 shiso leaves, minced

1 teaspoon toasted sesame oil

1 teaspoon honey

1/2 teaspoon dried red chile flakes

Peanut oil, for sautéing

2 tablespoons finely chopped fresh mint leaves, for garnish

Preheat the oven to 450°F. Prepare an ovenproof baking pan with a wire rack set inside, large enough for both racks of lamb.

To prepare the lamb, place a very large cast iron or heavy-bottomed sauté pan over high heat. Season the lamb racks with salt and pepper. Rub with canola oil. When the pan is hot, sear both racks of lamb on all sides for about 2 minutes per side, until very brown. Transfer to the prepared wire rack. Place the lamb racks in the oven for 8 minutes, until golden brown. Remove from the oven and set aside at room temperature to cool.

In a bowl, combine the wasabi, eggs, bread crumbs, and garlic confit and mix well to form a paste. Cover with plastic wrap.

On a large, smooth surface, dust the seared lamb with flour, rubbing the flour into the meat part of the lamb to form an even coat. Press a 1/4-inch layer of the paste over the lamb racks to form a crust, coating the entire rack. Transfer the lamb to a flat baking pan, and place the pan, uncovered, in the refrigerator until ready to roast.

To prepare the ginger mint syrup, place a saucepan over medium-low heat. Add the ginger, vinegar, honey, shallot, apple juice, salt, peppercorns, and mint. Cook for 15 minutes, stirring occasionally, until it becomes slightly syrupy. Strain through a chinois into a bowl.

Prepare a plate with several layers of paper towels.

To prepare the soba noodle cakes, place a large pot of salted water over high heat and bring to a boil. Add the soba noodles and cook for about 2 minutes, or until al dente. Remove from the heat and transfer the noodles to a colander and drain. Pour the soy sauce into a bowl, add the cornstarch, and whisk

until dissolved. Add the eggs, green onions, shiso leaves, sesame oil, honey, and chile flakes. Mix well. Fold in the cooked soba noodles. Place a large, non-stick skillet over medium-high heat and add a thin layer of peanut oil. Using a long-tined fork or tongs, twist 12 small mounds of the noodle mixture to create little cakes. When the oil is hot, sauté 4 of the soba cakes at a time, for 2 minutes on each side, until brown and crisp. Transfer the noodle cakes to the paper towels and drain.

Decrease the oven temperature to 375°F.

Remove the lamb from the refrigerator, and place in the oven. Roast for 15 minutes, until medium rare. Remove from the oven and let rest for 5 minutes.

To assemble the dish, place 2 noodle cakes on each of 6 dinner plates. Stir the mint for the garnish into the syrup, and mizzle it around the cakes on the plate. Using a thin, sharp knife, cut between the lamb bones, creating one double chop and one single chop, 3 bones per serving. Set a chop on each noodle cake, and serve immediately.

Mushroom and Marrow Crusted Strip Steak with Green Peppercorn Sauce and Fondant Potatoes

Serves 4

This is a dish for meat lovers. It's one of those robust, you-know-you've-been-fed meals: a thick juicy steak encrusted with meaty mushrooms and roasted bone marrow, surrounded by potatoes cooked in veal glace, all of it aswim in an ultra-rich, velvety sauce. I like to use prime meat that has been aged, especially with strip steak, where tenderness is important. You'll find that strip steak, when served medium rare, has a superb texture. If bone marrow is too hard to acquire in your locality, the recipe can be made without it, and you will still have a wonderful result.

GREEN PEPPERCORN SAUCE

1 tablespoon canola oil

$^1/_2$ cup diced yellow onion

$^1/_4$ cup peeled diced carrot

$^1/_4$ cup diced leek

3 cloves garlic, bruised

1 tablespoon tomato paste

1 teaspoon chopped fresh rosemary

$^1/_2$ cup mushroom scraps or stems, cleaned well

1 shallot, sliced

2 bay leaves

2 cups big red wine such as cabernet or Burgundy

8 cups veal stock (page 216)

2 tablespoons green peppercorns, rinsed well

MUSHROOM CRUST

3 pounds veal marrow bones, cut into 4-inch pieces

Canola oil

Kosher salt

Freshly ground black pepper

1 pound cremini mushrooms

2 tablespoons unsalted butter

2 tablespoons minced shallot

1 teaspoon balsamic vinegar

1 cup dry white wine

FONDANT POTATOES

8 medium russet potatoes, about 3 pounds

$^1/_4$ cup canola oil

Kosher salt

Freshly ground black pepper

3 cups veal stock (page 216)

8 cups water

3 tablespoons kosher salt

2 heads baby bok choy

4 trimmed, well-marbled strip steaks, 12 ounces each

Kosher salt

Freshly ground black pepper

Canola oil, for rubbing on steaks

1 tablespoon light olive oil

To prepare the sauce, place a large saucepan over medium heat, add the canola oil, and sauté the onions, carrots, leeks, and garlic for about 10 minutes, until they become a deep golden brown. Add the tomato paste and stir gently, coating all the vegetables. Cook for about 2 minutes, or until the tomato paste begins to brown slightly. Add the rosemary, mushroom scraps, shallot, bay leaves, and red wine. Cook for about 10 minutes, until the wine is reduced by half. Add the veal stock, decrease the heat to medium-low, and simmer the sauce for about 20 minutes, until reduced down to about half its original volume. Strain the sauce through a chinois into a large, clean saucepan.

Place the saucepan over medium heat for about 10 more minutes and reduce the sauce by half, or until it begins to thicken just slightly. The sauce should have a syrupy but not thick consistency. Strain through a fine chinois into a bowl. Stir in the green peppercorns. Keep warm.

Preheat the oven to 450°F.

To prepare the mushroom crust, place the marrow bones in a baking pan, rub with canola oil, and liberally salt and pepper them. Place the pan in the oven and roast for 30 minutes, until dark golden brown. Remove from the oven, and set aside until cool enough to handle. Cut around the inside of the bone and remove the marrow, pushing it out with your finger or a dowel; transfer it to a cutting board. Reserve the bones for stock.

Chop the marrow with a knife until it resembles a smooth paste. Place the mushrooms in a food processor and process until finely ground. Place a sauté pan over medium heat and add the butter. When it begins to brown, add the ground mushrooms, shallots, vinegar, and white wine. Cook for about 10 minutes, until no liquid is visible in the pan. Add the marrow and mix until completely combined. Remove from the heat and let cool.

Preheat the oven to 400°F.

To prepare the fondant potatoes, cut the potatoes in half lengthwise and tournée them (page 219) or simply peel them. Keep them immersed in water as you work, to prevent browning.

Place a roasting pan in the oven for 5 minutes.

Drain the potatoes well, and pat dry with a paper towel. Remove the roasting pan from the oven, and, taking care that the oil does not sputter, very slowly pour in the canola oil and add the potatoes.

Season the potatoes with the salt and pepper, return the pan to the oven, and roast them in the oil for 10 minutes, or until golden brown. Remove from the oven, add 1 cup of the veal stock, and return to the oven for 25 minutes, or until the potatoes are easily pierced with a knife.

While the potatoes are roasting, blanch the bok choy. Pour the water into a saucepan and add the salt. Bring to a boil over high heat. Fill a bowl with ice water. Blanch the bok choy in the boiling water for about 2 minutes. Using a slotted spoon or strainer, transfer the bok choy to the ice water bath. Shock for about 1 minute, or until thoroughly chilled. Immediately transfer to a colander and drain. Transfer to a work surface and split each head of bok choy in half lengthwise.

Place a small saucepan over medium heat, add the remaining 2 cups of veal stock, and cook for 5 minutes, until the liquid is reduced to $1/4$ cup and is quite thick. Remove from the heat.

After removing the potatoes from the oven, use a slotted spoon to transfer them to a plate. Brush the potatoes with the thick stock and cover with plastic wrap. Leave the oven at 400°F.

To prepare the steaks, heat a cast iron skillet over high heat. Season the steaks on all sides with salt and pepper, and rub with a small amount of canola oil. Sear the meat in the pan, turning once, for about 2 minutes per side. Place the steaks on a wire rack, with a pan underneath to catch the-

juices. Spread the mushroom-marrow mixture on top of the steaks. Bake in the oven for 8 to 10 minutes, until the crust browns and the steaks reach medium rare, or the desired doneness.

Place a sauté pan over medium-high heat and add the olive oil. Add the bok choy and quickly sauté for 2 minutes, until heated through but still crunchy. Season with salt.

To assemble the dish, place 4 potatoes on each plate. Lay a half head of bok choy on the potatoes, and set the steak atop. Ladle the sauce over all and serve immediately.

Stuffed Roasted Loin of Lamb with Leek Fondue and Yukon Gold Potato Quiche

Serves 4

When my wife, Jeanne, and I lived near Lancaster, Pennsylvania, the Amish farm capital of the United States, we used to get the biggest kick out of driving past those lush, green farms in the spring and seeing a flock of tiny lambs romping and leaping about, and sometimes a little boy or two running along with them. I think the natural way these lamb are raised has a lot to do with why their meat tastes so good. I can remember, as a fifteen-year-old busboy working at an Italian restaurant about a mile from my house, being totally intrigued with the elderly chef and owner, Aldo DeCarlo. He gave me my first taste of lamb that wasn't braised in some sort of tomato sauce. Instead, the lamb was roasted with oregano, olive oil, and garlic. It was fantastic. I used to watch for the lamb to be delivered to the restaurant from these farms, getting hopeful and excited to maybe have another taste, because the usual fare for a fifteen-year-old busboy was a plate of spaghetti and meatballs—a whole other love story.

You will need a ball of butcher's twine to tie the lamb roulade, and a mandoline to slice the potatoes thin enough for the quiche.

SPINACH STUFFING

2 tablespoons extra virgin olive oil

1 pound baby spinach leaves, washed and dried

Pinch of salt

Pinch of freshly ground black pepper

1/4 cup garlic confit (page 208)

2 boneless lamb loins, fully trimmed, silver skin removed, about 4 pounds

2 tablespoons fresh marjoram leaves

Kosher salt

Freshly ground black pepper

YUKON GOLD POTATO QUICHE

1 tablespoon unsalted butter

1/4 cup finely diced yellow onions

1/2 cup chopped fresh parsley leaves

1 tablespoon minced garlic

2 cups half-and-half

6 eggs

2 tablespoons Dijon mustard

1 teaspoon salt

1/4 teaspoon freshly ground nutmeg

1 cup grated Parmesan cheese

3 large Yukon Gold potatoes

LEEK FONDUE

2 tablespoons unsalted butter

2 cups diced leek, white part only

1/2 cup dry white wine

1/2 cup blonde chicken stock (page 213)

2 tablespoons heavy cream

Kosher salt

Freshly ground white pepper

Light olive oil, for searing lamb

4 sprigs marjoram, for garnish

To prepare the spinach stuffing, place a large sauté pan over medium heat and add the olive oil. Add the spinach, salt, and pepper and sauté for about 1 minute, until wilted. Drain well in a colander, gently pressing out the excess juice. Transfer to a bowl and mix in the garlic confit. Set the bowl over ice water to chill.

To prepare the lamb, cut the lamb loins lengthwise, two-thirds of the way through, creating an open flap. With a meat pounder or the flat side of a cleaver, lightly pound the meat until it is all of equal thickness, about $1/2$ inch thick. Press the marjoram, salt, and pepper into the flesh. Divide the spinach stuffing in half, and lay a strip of it in the center of the cut side of each of the flattened lamb loins. Roll one end over the filling, and continue to roll tightly, creating a roulade. Repeat with the other lamb loin.

Tie butcher's twine around the loins at 2-inch intervals to hold them together. Wrap the loins in plastic wrap and refrigerate.

Preheat the oven to 350°F. Lightly butter a 9 by 9-inch nonreactive baking dish.

To prepare the potato quiche, place a sauté pan over medium heat and add the butter. Add the onion, parsley, and garlic and sauté for about 3 minutes, until soft. Remove from the heat. In a large mixing bowl, whisk together the half-and-half, eggs, mustard, salt, nutmeg, and Parmesan cheese. Peel the potatoes and slice them very thinly on the mandoline. Immediately place the potatoes into the egg mixture. Add the onion mixture and fold all the ingredients together thoroughly and gently, making sure to coat all the slices of the potato with the quiche mixture. Pour the quiche into the baking dish and place in the center of the oven.

Bake for 15 minutes, uncovered, until the surface is golden. Remove from the oven. Cover with aluminum foil, and return to the oven for 45 minutes, or until a knife inserted in the center comes out clean. Remove from the oven and set in a warm place.

To prepare the fondue, place a saucepan over medium heat and add the butter. When the butter has melted, add the leeks and sauté for about 4 minutes, until soft. Add the white wine, chicken stock, cream, salt, and pepper. Cook for 5 minutes, until the mixture bubbles and thickens. Remove from the heat and set in a warm place.

Preheat the oven to 400°F.

To finish the lamb, remove the lamb from the refrigerator. Place a heavy-bottomed cast iron skillet over high heat. Season the outside of the lamb roulades with salt and pepper. Heat a thin layer of oil in the skillet, add the lamb, and completely sear each side and the ends of the lamb loins for about 2 minutes per side, until nicely browned.

Place the lamb in the oven for 10 minutes, until medium rare, or to your liking.

Remove the lamb from the oven, and let rest for 5 minutes. Cut off the string with scissors. Keep the roulades warm on the surface of the stove.

Cut the potato quiche into 3-inch squares, and place a square on each dinner plate. Spoon some of the leek fondue next to the quiche. Carve the lamb into 1-inch slices, and place the slices on the potatoes and leeks. Garnish with the marjoram sprigs. Serve immediately.

"Quick" Braised Rabbit Saddle with Matzo Scallion Dumplings and Fresh Soybeans

Serves 4

Braising is a technique involving long, slow cooking in liquid that develops flavor and tenderizes by gently breaking down tough fibers. The reason we "quick" braise is that rabbit is a very lean meat, and the saddle is an especially lean cut. I remember making fricassee de lapin, rabbit stew, as an apprentice; the flavor was always savory and delicious, and though some of the rabbit was moist, the tender pieces leaned toward the dry side. This dish creates a rich braising sauce yet preserves the tenderness of the rabbit. I adore matzo balls, and that's basically what these dumplings are, with a little herb and green onion added to give them a more intense flavor.

3 pounds fresh rabbit saddle, cut into 3-inch portions, bones scraped

2 cups buttermilk

MATZO SCALLION DUMPLINGS

1 cup matzo meal

1 teaspoon salt

$1/2$ teaspoon freshly ground white pepper

4 eggs, beaten

$1/4$ cup blonde chicken stock (page 213)

2 tablespoons unsalted clarified butter (page 206)

1 tablespoon chopped fresh dill

1 tablespoon chopped fresh chives

2 tablespoons chopped fresh Italian parsley

$1/2$ cup chopped green onion, white part only

$1/2$ cup all-purpose flour

Kosher salt

Freshly ground black pepper

$1/4$ cup light olive oil

$1/2$ cup finely diced yellow onion

2 tablespoons finely diced shallot

1 tablespoon minced garlic

6 juniper berries

1 tablespoon tomato paste

2 cups dry red wine

6 cups brown chicken stock (page 214)

1 bouquet garni (page 205)

4 cups water

1 tablespoon kosher salt

8 ounces fresh, shelled soybeans (about 2 cups)

2 tablespoons unsalted butter

Pinch of salt

Pinch of freshly ground white pepper

Have your butcher cut the rabbit saddle and scrape the bones clean. Place the rabbit pieces in a large resealable bag, pour in the buttermilk, seal, and marinate for 4 hours in the refrigerator.

To prepare the matzo dumplings, combine the matzo meal, salt, and white pepper in a bowl and whisk together. In a separate bowl, whisk together the eggs, chicken stock, butter, dill, chives, parsley, and green onions. Pour the liquid mixture into the matzo meal and blend just until the dry ingredients are moistened. Cover and refrigerate for about 1 hour.

Bring a large pot of lightly salted water to a boil over medium-high heat. Set out a piece of wax paper and a buttered plate.

Lightly form the dumplings between your palms, rolling the dough into 1-inch long by $1/2$-inch thick football shapes, and place them on the wax paper. When all the dumplings have been formed, drop them gently, one by one, into the boiling

water. Decrease the heat to medium-low and cook for 15 minutes, or until they rise to the top. Using a spider, gently lift them out of the pot, transfer to the plate, and cover.

Place the flour in a shallow bowl.

To braise the rabbit, remove the bag of marinated rabbit pieces from the refrigerator, and remove the pieces from the marinade. Transfer to a colander and drain. Salt and pepper the pieces and dredge them in the flour.

Place a heavy-bottomed pot or Dutch oven over medium heat and add the oil. When the oil is hot, add the pieces of rabbit and sear for about 1 minute per side, until golden brown. Transfer the rabbit pieces to a plate.

Place the onion, shallot, garlic, and juniper berries in the hot oil and sauté for about 3 minutes, until they begin to brown. Add the tomato paste, and sauté for another 2 minutes, until the tomato paste begins to brown. Add the red wine and simmer for about 10 minutes, until reduced by half. Add the brown chicken stock and bouquet garni. Decrease the heat to medium-low and simmer for about 30 minutes, until reduced by one-third.

While the sauce is simmering, blanch the soybeans. Pour the water into a saucepan and add the salt. Bring to a boil over high heat. Fill a bowl with ice water. Blanch the soybeans in the boiling water for 2 minutes. Using a slotted spoon or strainer, transfer the soybeans to the ice water bath. Shock for about 1 minute, or until cold. Immediately transfer to a colander and drain. Transfer to a bowl and cover.

Add the rabbit pieces to the sauce and simmer in the braising liquid for 20 minutes, until tender when pierced with a fork. Using a slotted spoon, carefully transfer the rabbit to a plate.

Continue to simmer the sauce for about 10 minutes, or until reduced by a third. Strain through a chinois into a clean saucepan.

Return the rabbit pieces to the sauce and place over very low heat to keep warm.

Warm 4 dinner plates.

Place a sauté pan over medium heat and add the butter. When the butter has melted, add the soybeans and sauté for 2 minutes, until tender. Add the matzo dumplings and sauté for an additional 2 minutes, until heated through. Season with salt and white pepper. Remove from the heat.

To serve, apportion the dumplings and soybeans equally among the warm plates. Place pieces of rabbit on each plate, and generously ladle the sauce over the top. Serve immediately.

Grilled Rack of Lamb with a Creamy Compote of Fingerling Potatoes, Bacon, and Sweet Corn

Serves 4

For this dish, we "lollipop" the lamb: kitchen lingo for a technique similar to frenching, which involves removing any sinew or excess fat on the lamb chop, and exposing a large portion of the bone, creating a sort of lollipop of lamb. Unless you are familiar with this technique, you may want to ask your butcher to do this part for you. We marinate the chops for a few hours, then cook them very quickly over a hot grill and serve them on a compote that reminds me of a creamy, hot, potato salad. A special ingredient that gives this dish a beautiful, smoky flavor is Nueske's applewood-smoked bacon (see page 220). I have used this bacon from the first day I tasted it; I know of nothing that compares in quality and flavor. This is a substantial, hearty dish and a regular player on the Geronimo menu.

$1/4$ cup light olive oil

1 tablespoon minced lemon zest

2 tablespoons minced garlic

2 tablespoons minced fresh rosemary leaves

2 tablespoons minced fresh mint leaves

1 tablespoon freshly ground black pepper

2 racks of lamb, 8 bones each, cut into 16 lollipops

POTATO COMPOTE

About $1^1/2$ pounds fingerling potatoes

2 tablespoons unsalted butter

$1/2$ cup diced high-quality bacon

1 teaspoon kosher salt

$1/2$ cup sweet corn kernels, about 1 ear

2 tablespoons very finely diced red onion

1 teaspoon minced garlic

$1/4$ cup very finely diced cornichon

$1/4$ cup very finely diced peeled carrot

$1/2$ cup brown chicken stock (page 214)

$1/2$ cup heavy cream

$1/2$ cup milk

$1/2$ teaspoon freshly ground white pepper

Kosher salt

High-quality extra virgin olive oil, for drizzling

8 mint sprigs, for garnish

To marinate the lamb, in a small bowl, mix together the olive oil, lemon zest, garlic, rosemary, mint, and pepper. Arrange the lamb chops on their sides in a baking pan. Pour the marinade over the meat of the chops and rub it thoroughly into the flesh. Cover and marinate in the refrigerator for 3 hours.

To prepare the potatoes, place the potatoes in a pot of salted water to cover. Place over medium-high heat and bring to a boil. Cook until tender when pierced with a fork. Remove from the heat. Transfer to a colander and drain. Allow to cool to room temperature. Transfer to a cutting surface and slice in half lengthwise. Place a large sauté pan over medium heat and add the butter, bacon, and salt. Cook for about 5 minutes, until the bacon begins to brown. Add the cooked potatoes, corn, red onion, garlic, cornichon, and carrot. Stir gently with a wooden spoon until all the ingredients are combined. Add the chicken stock, cream, milk, and white pepper. Decrease the heat to low. Simmer for about 10 minutes, until the liquid is thick and bubbly. Stir gently periodically, being careful not to mash the potatoes. Remove from the heat and keep warm.

Prepare a hot fire in a charcoal grill, or preheat a gas grill to high.

To grill the lamb, season both sides of the lamb lollipops with salt. Grill the lamb at the edge of the grill, with the meat part over the direct flame, because direct fire under the bones will cause them to burn and break. Don't worry if they do burn a bit. They will still be delicious; they just won't look as nice. Cook the lamb for about 2 minutes per side for medium rare, or to your desired doneness.

To serve, place a mound of the potatoes in the center of each of 4 plates and arrange 4 lamb lollipops around the base of the potato mound, with the bones sticking straight up, so that they can be grabbed and eaten. Drizzle a small amount of olive oil over the plate. Garnish with sprigs of mint, and serve immediately.

Chicken in a Chanterelle Mushroom and Garlic Stew

Serves 4

This recipe is actually a version of coq au vin: chicken in wine sauce with mushrooms. Instead of using white field mushrooms, I use chanterelles, which lend the dish a unique flavor and texture, as does the addition of potatoes. There is always a special place in my heart for potatoes cooked in a hearty sauce: they remind me of pot roasts my mother made, simmering all day on the stove until the potatoes almost fell apart because they were so deliciously loaded with the sauce.

We use chicken from Pollo Real here in New Mexico (see page 220). This recipe can be made a day ahead and brought up to serving temperature over low heat.

4 skinless, bone-in chicken breasts halves, with frenched wing attached (page 219)

Kosher salt

Freshly cracked black pepper

1 cup all-purpose flour

Canola oil, for sautéing

2 tablespoons unsalted butter

2 slices smoked bacon, finely diced

2 pounds fresh chanterelle mushrooms, trimmed and sliced in half

1/4 cup sliced shallot

12 cloves garlic, cut in half lengthwise

2 tablespoons tomato paste

3 cups dry red wine

4 bay leaves

2 sprigs rosemary

2 tablespoons minced fresh chives

12 cups brown chicken stock (page 214)

20 potatoes, tournéed (page 219)

White truffle oil, for drizzling

Fleur de sel

Season the chicken breasts with salt and cracked pepper. Place the flour in a shallow bowl, and dredge the breasts in the flour.

Heat a large sautoir, or high-walled skillet, over medium-high heat. Cover the bottom of the pan with a thin layer of canola oil.

When the oil is hot, sauté the floured chicken breasts, turning once, for about 2 minutes per side, until browned. Transfer to a plate. Place the butter, bacon, mushrooms, shallot, and garlic in the skillet and sauté over medium heat for about 5 minutes, stirring frequently, until they begin to brown.

Add the tomato paste and cook, stirring, for 2 minutes, until the tomato paste begins to brown. Decrease the heat to medium-low. Add the red wine, bay leaves, rosemary sprigs, and chives. Simmer for 20 minutes, until the wine is reduced by half.

Place a large saucepan over medium heat. Pour in the chicken stock and bring to a simmer. Simmer for about 30 minutes, or until the stock is reduced by half. Remove from the heat. Add the stock, chicken breasts, and potatoes to the stew and cover. Decrease the heat to medium-low and cook for about 30 minutes, or until the potatoes are tender and the chicken is fully cooked.

Serve in the sautoir, family style, with a generous drizzle of truffle oil and a few pinches of fleur de sel over the top.

Sautéed Pheasant with Figs, White Yams, Country Ham, and Fig Brandy Sauce

Serves 4

In Pennsylvania, during pheasant season, a group of hunting friends of mine used to give me a bird or two to cook. A couple of times, I actually even tagged along to hunting camp with them. They always swore they came to hunt, and this they did, but eating was also pretty high on the daily priority list. They would bring along boxes of hickory-smoked hams, sausages, white tail deer bologna: nearly every kind of cured meat you could name. We would get up at the crack of dawn for huge breakfasts, cooked over an old wood-burning stove, in ancient, well-seasoned Griswolds. They would pour a sweet fig conserve and maple syrup over ham steaks. We seemed to have that with every meal. I can still taste those enticing sweet flavors, mingled with the smokiness from the ham. In this dish, we combine smoked country ham with a sweet fig port sauce, and they make a potent and delectable marriage with the pheasant and fresh figs. It's important to cook the pheasant, especially the breast, very carefully, to preserve the moisture in this lean, delicate meat.

4 skin-on pheasant breast halves, 6 ounces each, frenched (page 219)

4 teaspoons unsalted butter

1 tablespoon sliced shallot

4 small sprigs rosemary

Kosher salt

Freshly ground black pepper

FIG BRANDY SAUCE

1 teaspoon light olive oil

10 fresh, ripe figs, halved

6 dried figs, halved

1 teaspoon minced white onion

1 sprig thyme

1/8 teaspoon ground cinnamon

10 black peppercorns

1/2 cup brandy

1 cup veal demi-glace (page 212)

1/2 cup veal stock (page 216)

Kosher salt

1 tablespoon unsalted butter

WHITE YAMS WITH PARSLEY

1 large white yam (to yield about 2 cups when diced)

2 tablespoons unsalted butter

1/2 teaspoon kosher salt

1/2 cup chopped, fresh Italian parsley

1 tablespoon real maple syrup

Canola oil, for serving

12 slices smoked ham, 1/8 inch thick

1/4 cup real maple syrup

8 fresh figs, sliced, for garnish

4 sprigs rosemary, for garnish

To prepare the pheasant, place 1 teaspoon of the butter, along with one-fourth of the shallots and a rosemary sprig, under the skin of each breast. Season the pheasant with salt and pepper. Transfer to a plate, cover and refrigerate.

To prepare the sauce, place a saucepan over medium heat and add the olive oil. When the oil is hot, add the fresh figs, dried figs, onion, thyme, cinnamon, and peppercorns. Cook, stirring frequently, for about 5 minutes, until the figs begin to break

down. Add the brandy, and flambé, by igniting the alcohol and allowing it to burn off. When the flame dissipates, add the demi-glace and veal stock. Simmer for 5 minutes, or until thickened slightly. Remove from the heat. Press the sauce through a sturdy, large-holed, chinois into a bowl. Strain again through a fine chinois into a bowl. Check the seasoning for salt. Stir in the butter. Cover and set aside in a warm place.

To prepare the yams, place a pot of salted water over high heat and bring to a boil. Add the yam and cook until tender when pierced with a fork. Remove from the heat, transfer to a colander, and drain. Place on a cutting surface and cut into a large dice. Place a large sauté pan over medium heat and add the butter. When the butter begins to bubble, add the cooked yams and salt. Sauté for 5 minutes, until heated through. Add the parsley and maple syrup, and cook for 1 minute, until nicely glazed. Remove from the heat, and set aside in a warm place.

Preheat the oven to 375°F.

To cook the pheasant, pour a small layer of canola oil in the bottom of an ovenproof sauté pan, and place over medium-high heat. When the oil is hot, sear the pheasant breasts, skin side down first, for 2 minutes per side, until golden brown on both sides. Drain the excess oil. Place the whole pan in the oven and roast for 10 minutes, until cooked. Remove the pan from the oven, place 3 ham slices atop each pheasant breast, and drizzle the maple syrup over the ham. Return the pan to the oven for about 5 minutes, or until the pheasant is firm to the touch.

To assemble, divide the yams equally among 4 dinner plates. At Geronimo, we use 3-inch ring molds and gently press the potatoes down, forming a nicely rounded cake. Place 3 slices of the ham over the potatoes, then, a layer of fresh fig slices, and finally, top with the pheasant breast. Pour the sauce around the yams. Garnish with more fig slices and a sprig of rosemary. Serve immediately.

Pan-Roasted Guinea Hen Breasts with Shrimp Ravioli and Fresh Basil Shallot Coulis

Serves 4

Americans seldom think of guinea hen as a household staple. In Italy and France, however, it's truly admired. The meat has a delicious flavor, though it is very lean and needs to be cooked carefully so it will remain moist. For this recipe, I sear the breasts until the skin is crispy and then roast them in the oven for a short time. Unlike chicken breast, the breast of the guinea hen can be served slightly pink. The combination of the shrimp ravioli and the fresh basil beautifully accents the rich taste of the hen and creates a unique dish. The pasta dough will need to rest for 1 hour before you make the ravioli.

BASIL SHALLOT COULIS

$^2/_3$ cup good-quality extra virgin olive oil

1 teaspoon minced garlic

1 cup sliced shallot

$^1/_4$ cup vermouth

$1^1/_2$ cups fresh basil leaves

2 tablespoons chopped fresh Italian parsley

$^1/_2$ cup cold water

SHRIMP RAVIOLI

2 pounds shelled, deveined raw shrimp

$^1/_2$ teaspoon crustacean spice (page 206)

1 tablespoon unsalted butter

$^1/_2$ cup very finely diced leek

$^1/_2$ teaspoon minced garlic

1 egg

1 teaspoon water

1 recipe pasta dough, made with tomato paste
   (variation, page 210)

1 tablespoon light olive oil

4 skin-on whole guinea hen breasts halved, 6 ounces each

Kosher salt

Freshly ground white pepper

Light olive oil, for searing

Fried shallots (page 208), for garnish

Pea shoots, for garnish

To prepare the coulis, place a saucepan over low heat and add the olive oil, garlic, shallots, and vermouth. Cook for about 5 minutes, until the shallots are translucent. Remove from the heat. Combine the basil leaves and parsley in a blender, and pour the warm oil and shallot mixture over them. Purée until smooth. Add the water, and press the mixture through a tamis into a metal bowl. Fill a larger bowl with ice water, and set the coulis over the ice bath to cool.

To prepare the ravioli filling, cut the shrimp in half lengthwise and cut the halves into small slices. Season the shrimp pieces with the crustacean spice. Place a sauté pan over medium heat, and add the butter. When the butter begins bubbling, add the shrimp, leeks, and garlic. Cook, stirring frequently, for about 3 minutes, until the shrimp are just barely done. Keep in mind that some residual cooking will occur after you take the shrimp off the heat. Drain the shrimp in a colander placed over a bowl. Reserve the juices for later use.

Whisk together the egg and water.

To assemble and cook the ravioli, roll the pasta dough out on a lightly floured surface to a thickness of about $^1/_{16}$ inch, or use the ravioli setting on your pasta machine. Using a 3-inch fluted or plain-edged round cookie cutter, cut out 24 circles of pasta.

Brush 12 circles with the egg wash. Place equal amounts of the shrimp mixture in the middle of each circle. Center the other 12 circles atop the filling. Press gently to push out any air, and seal the edges. Cover with a slightly damp towel.

Bring a pot of salted water to a boil over high heat. Add the ravioli to the water and cook for about 3 minutes, or until they float to the top. Remove from the heat. Using a slotted spoon or spider, transfer the ravioli to a bowl. Place a sauté pan over medium heat and add the olive oil and the reserved juice from the cooked shrimp. Sauté the ravioli for 1 minute, until heated through. Remove from the heat and keep warm.

Preheat the oven to 400°F.

To prepare the guinea hen, make sure the skin of the breast halves is dry to attain the best crispness, and season with salt and white pepper. Place an ovenproof sauté pan over medium-high heat, and pour a thin layer of olive oil into the pan. When the oil is hot, sear the meat, skin-side down first, for 2 minutes per side, until golden brown. Place the pan in the oven for 10 minutes, for a slightly pink interior, or longer if desired.

To assemble the dish, place a ravioli in the center of the plate. Place a half hen breast over the ravioli and repeat, adding another layer, finishing with a ravioli on top. Spoon the coulis around the base of the stack, and garnish with the fried shallots and pea shoots. Serve immediately.

Sautéed Squab Breasts with Braised Baby Fennel and Sun-Dried Cherry Sauce

Serves 4

The meat of squabs, which are young pigeons, is delicate and extremely tender, with a pleasing, gamelike taste. Squabs are best served medium rare or, at very most, cooked just to medium. Their taste and texture change drastically when overcooked: the meat becomes grainy and tastes almost like chicken liver. You will need some butcher's twine for this recipe, because we tie the squab breasts to keep them a uniform size. This protects the small end of the breast from becoming overcooked.

The sweet and sour notes of the sauce complement this delectable pairing of flavorful meat and braised fennel. I serve this with a simple, crispy rösti potato cake, a Swiss version of potato pancakes. You will need cheesecloth to prepare the potatoes.

12 skin-on whole squab breasts with frenched wing attached, halved, about 5-ounces each (page 219)

2 tablespoons fresh thyme leaves

2 tablespoons minced shallot

1/8 teaspoon ground cinnamon

BRAISED BABY FENNEL

2 whole baby fennel bulbs, trimmed

1 diced yellow onion

1 slice applewood-smoked bacon

1 sprig thyme

About 6 cups blonde chicken stock (page 213)

Kosher salt

Freshly ground white pepper

SUN-DRIED CHERRY SAUCE

1 cup sun-dried cherries

1 cup port wine

1 cup water

1/2 cup red wine, such as Burgundy

2 tablespoons sliced shallot

1 teaspoon grated orange zest

1 cup veal demi-glace (page 212)

Kosher salt

Freshly ground white pepper

2 tablespoons unsalted butter

POTATO RÖSTI

1 pound Yukon Gold potatoes, peeled and shredded

1 small white onion, shredded

Kosher salt

Freshly ground black pepper

1/4 cup cooked and diced applewood-smoked bacon

1 teaspoon fresh thyme leaves

Canola oil, for sautéing

Kosher salt

Freshly ground black pepper

Canola oil, for sautéing

To prepare the squab, remove the cartilage from each breast half. Lay the 8 individual half-breasts, skin side down, on a clean surface.

Sprinkle the thyme, shallot, and cinnamon on the inside of the squab breasts. Roll the breasts up into a small spool, skin side out. Tie a length of butcher's twine around each one. Transfer to a plate. Cover and refrigerate.

To braise the fennel, place a saucepan over medium-high heat and add the fennel, onion, bacon, thyme, and enough chicken stock to cover. Bring to a simmer, and cover with a lid. Cook for

30 minutes, or until a knife easily pierces the fennel bulbs. Remove from the heat and set aside in a warm place.

To prepare the cherry sauce, place a saucepan over medium-low heat and add the sun-dried cherries, port, water, wine, shallot, and orange zest. Simmer for 15 minutes, until the cherries are softened and the liquid has reduced by half. Remove from the heat, transfer the sauce to a blender and purée until smooth. Strain the mixture through a medium-gauge chinois into a clean saucepan. Place the saucepan over medium-low heat. Add the demi-glace. Simmer for 5 minutes, until the flavors meld. Skim off any impurities that may rise to the top. Strain through a fine chinois into a bowl. Season to taste with salt and white pepper. Whisk the butter into the sauce. Set aside in a warm place.

Preheat the oven to 375°F.

To prepare the potatoes, combine the potatoes and onions in a bowl, and liberally salt and pepper them. Wrap them in cheesecloth. Over the sink, squeeze and drain off any excess water. Return the potatoes and onions to the bowl and gently stir in the bacon and thyme leaves.

Prepare a plate with several layers of paper towels.

Pour a layer of the canola oil into a cast iron or heavy-bottomed skillet, and place over medium heat. Divide the potato mixture into 4 cakes, 1 inch thick. When the oil is hot, brown them evenly on both sides, for about 2 minutes per side. Set them in a baking pan, and bake for 8 to 10 minutes, until the potatoes are fully cooked. Remove from the oven. Transfer to the paper towels and drain. Set in a warm place.

To sauté the squab, salt and pepper the rolled-up breasts. Place an ovenproof sauté pan over medium-high heat and add the oil. When the oil is hot, sauté the squab, turning frequently, for about 2 minutes, until all the sides are golden brown. Drain off the oil and place the pan in the oven for about 3 minutes, until the squab is cooked to medium rare. Remove from the oven. Carefully cut away the string and discard. Set the squab in a warm place.

To serve, place a potato rösti on each of 4 dinner plates. For each serving, cut 2 of the spools of squab breast into several slices and stack the slices on top of the potato cake. Lean another breast piece, uncut, against each stack. Remove the fennel bulbs from the stock, cut the fennel bulbs in half and pare out the core. Season with the salt and white pepper, and lean 1 half of the fennel against the other side of the stack. Spoon a puddle of sauce around the potato rösti, and serve immediately.

I was going to name the restaurant Cañon.

We had all the artwork created and stationery printed. We were getting ready to open, when, at the last second, Patricia and her partner decided I would have to buy the

Cliff on . . . a Rose by Any Other Name

building as well as the restaurant.

I only had a certain amount of cash, and it was going to take everything I had.

I was drinking a beer at Tesuque Village Market and noticed a picture of Geronimo, the great Apache warrior, hanging on the wall. Suddenly, I realized I didn't like the name Cañon. I liked the name Geronimo.

Seeing the photograph of the heroic chief reminded me of that wild call you make when you jump out of an airplane, Geronimooooooo. That's why, in our logo, the "o" is placed as if it's falling.

I'd worked many years in the restaurant business, doing everything I could to gain financial ground. Now this project had become so huge that I had just enough money to buy the restaurant and the building, and just barely enough to open the restaurant. I was doing this by the skin of my teeth.

The restaurant was in operation as The Borrego House, and I thought it best to stay open in November and December for the holidays. Coyote Café was going to do a big Christmas party here, to help me get started. After that, I'd close down in January for about three weeks.

I began telling people that I was going to name my new restaurant Geronimo. We eventually opened as Geronimo Lodge.

There was a lot of controversy about it. People were saying, "You're out of your mind. First of all, it's a stupid name for a restaurant. Second of all, he was an Apache, and that

has nothing to do with Santa Fe." Native Americans were writing me letters of protest, saying, "You're a white guy, using the name of an Indian. You're trying to make money off the Native Americans."

I kept explaining, "It isn't a reference to Geronimo, the Apache warrior." I started to get nervous, wondering if I should go back to the Cañon idea.

Wait, I thought, I *love* the name Geronimo. I think it's right. It fits.

The next Monday, I was up on a ladder, painting the ceiling. I painted the whole building myself, because I couldn't afford to hire anybody.

I had been experimenting to find the color I wanted, taking the one wall and painting ten big stripes of a yellowish linen color. I sat there, looked at all the painted colors, and said, "That one, that's the one I like." I had just begun painting, when an old friend I hadn't seen in months walked in and called out, "Hey, Cliff, I have a *great* name for your restaurant." I said, "Oh, what's that?" He was holding a small book, and said very seriously, "I think you should call this restaurant Geronimo." "Ha, ha, really funny." I said. "You've heard all the talk about this, all the controversy." "No," he told me, "I don't know anything about that."

"I was reading this pamphlet about historic buildings in Santa Fe, and it says this building is known as the Borrego House, named after the socially prominent and political family who owned it from 1840 to 1900. But the building was actually built in 1756, by a man named Gerónimo Lopez."

I was shocked, stunned, I almost fell off the ladder. I ran out in the middle of the street, looked up at the building, and said, "Something's right, something's really right."

Napoleon of King Salmon with Braised Ruby Chard, Lemon Crêpes, and Green Chile Butter Sauce

Serves 4

Fresh-caught Alaskan king salmon is a prize. Wild king salmon has a high-fat, soft-textured flesh that ranges from off-white to bright red and is just loaded with flavor. One of my pet peeves is seeing these beautiful fish thrown around as though they were made of rubber, because they are actually very fragile. When you buy your salmon, make sure the flesh is treated gently and that there are no rips or separations in the meat. This is a fairly simple recipe that we make using New Mexico green chile from Hatch, a source of great pride in the state. The crêpes soak up the green chile sauce and act as a sort of a play on the white flour tortillas that we Santa Feans normally eat with chile sauce.

GREEN CHILE BUTTER SAUCE

1 cup white wine vinegar

2 tablespoons freshly squeezed lemon juice

1 shallot, sliced

1 clove garlic, bruised

1 bay leaf

1 sprig thyme

1¹/₂ cups unsalted butter, cut into 1-inch cubes and refrigerated

1 cup green chile purée (page 209)

Kosher salt

Freshly ground white pepper

LEMON CRÊPES

2 cups all-purpose flour

4 eggs

1 cup milk

1 cup water

2 tablespoons finely minced lemon zest

¹/₂ teaspoon lemon oil

¹/₂ teaspoon salt

¹/₄ cup butter, browned and kept warm

Canola oil, for oiling grill

8 medallions of king salmon, 3 ounces each

Kosher salt

Freshly ground white pepper

BRAISED RUBY CHARD

3 tablespoons light olive oil

¹/₂ cup finely sliced yellow onion

1 teaspoon minced garlic

Leaves from 2 bunches ruby chard

¹/₈ teaspoon freshly ground nutmeg

Kosher salt

Freshly ground white pepper

To prepare the sauce, place a saucepan over medium heat and add the vinegar, lemon juice, shallot, garlic, bay leaf, and thyme. Cook for 10 minutes, until the mixture is reduced to about ¹/₄ cup of liquid. Remove from the heat. Using a wooden spoon, stir in 4 cubes of the chilled butter until fully incorporated.

Place the pan back over low heat and stir in the remaining butter, a cube at a time, until fully incorporated. Add the green chile purée and fold in gently. Remove from the heat immediately. Strain through a chinois into a thick ceramic bowl. Season to taste with salt and white pepper. Set in a warm but not hot place, as too much heat will cause the emulsification to separate.

To prepare the crêpes, measure the flour into a bowl, and create a well in the center. In a separate bowl, combine the eggs, milk, water, lemon zest,

lemon oil, and salt and whisk together. Pour the liquid into the flour and whisk until smooth. Strain through a chinois into a bowl. Whisk in the browned butter. Cover and refrigerate for 1 hour, until thoroughly chilled.

Set out 2 clean kitchen towels.

If you own a crêpe maker, follow the manufacturer's instructions, or take a 6-inch nonstick pan and place it over medium-low heat. Using a 2-ounce ladle, pour the batter into the pan. Quickly lift it off the fire and tilt the pan in all directions, coating the bottom and sides of the pan with the batter. Place the pan back on the heat for about 30 seconds, until the edges of the crêpe brown slightly. Gently lift one edge, peel it back, and flip the crêpe onto its other side. Cook for 10 seconds and flip the crepe onto a clean towel. Usually the butter in the batter, along with using a nonstick pan, is enough to keep the crêpes from sticking. If not, spray the pan with a nonstick spray oil.

Continue making crêpes until all the batter is used. It should have more than you need. The remaining crêpes make a terrific breakfast with some Gruyère cheese and eggs.

Cut 4 of the crêpes into 4 triangles each, and cover with a damp towel.

Prepare a medium-hot fire in a charcoal grill, or preheat a gas grill to medium-high.

Oil the grate well to prevent sticking. Gently rub the salmon medallions with oil and season with salt and white pepper. Cover and refrigerate.

To prepare the chard, place a sauté pan over medium heat and add the olive oil. When the oil is hot, add the onion and garlic, and cook for about 2 minutes, until just slightly brown. Add the chard, nutmeg, and salt and white pepper to taste and cook, stirring frequently, for about 1 minute, just until the leaves begin to wilt. Remove from the heat and keep warm.

Warm a platter for the fish, along with 4 dinner plates.

Remove the salmon from the refrigerator and gently lay the medallions on the oiled grill. Cook for 2 minutes per side, turning once, until the flesh is medium rare. Transfer directly onto the warm platter.

To assemble, on each warmed dinner plate, mound a small bed of the chard. Place 2 crêpe triangles over the chard, then 1 medallion of salmon and repeat the process to form a stack. Ladle the chile sauce on top, as if you were pouring syrup over a stack of pancakes. Serve immediately.

Grilled King Salmon with Roasted Tomato Mousse and Poached Heirloom Baby Tomatoes

Serves 4

Through June, July, and August, we are privileged to have Alaskan king salmon on the menu. There is a considerable difference in flavor, color, and texture between the Atlantic salmon and these Alaskan kings. Their flesh is nearly crimson orange, sometimes even a deep scarlet, and very delicate. It is here at Geronimo, we grill them over mesquite charcoal and serve them on a bed of warm baby heirloom tomatoes, gently heated in olive oil that is drawn off from the garlic confit. We obtain our heirloom tomatoes from the Chef's Garden, a specialty produce company that grows heirloom fruit and vegetables of extraordinary flavor and quality (see page 200).

This is an ideal meal for a midsummer al fresco fiesta, served with some fresh, hot rolls and a little dish of the warm oil you have reserved after poaching the tomatoes.

ROASTED TOMATO MOUSSE

4 ripe Roma tomatoes, cored

$1/4$ teaspoon kosher salt, plus more for sprinkling over tomatoes

1 tablespoon minced shallot

1 tablespoon extra virgin olive oil

1 teaspoon vinegar

$1/4$ teaspoon sugar

2 tablespoons minced fresh basil

$1/2$ cup heavy cream

Pinch of freshly ground white pepper

POACHED TOMATOES

3 cups oil from garlic confit (page 208)

8 cups ripe peeled (page 219) and cored assorted baby heirloom tomatoes, about 2 pounds

4 pieces fresh king salmon fillet, 6 to 8 ounces each

Kosher salt

Canola oil, for rubbing on fish

Fleur de sel

1 cup micro (baby) greens, for garnish

Preheat the oven to 375°F.

Place a stainless steel bowl and whisk in the refrigerator to chill. Oil a baking sheet.

To prepare the mousse, wash the Roma tomatoes, and cut them in half. Sprinkle the cut sides with salt. Spread the tomatoes, cut sides down, on the baking sheet, and roast for 20 minutes, until they brown slightly. Remove from the oven. Transfer to a food processor, add the shallot, olive oil, vinegar, and sugar, and purée until smooth. Push the purée through a sieve into a glass or ceramic bowl, and stir in the basil.

In the chilled bowl, with the chilled whisk, whip the heavy cream, until it forms soft peaks. Gently fold in the tomato purée. Season with $1/4$ teaspoon salt and the white pepper. Cover and refrigerate.

Prepare a medium-hot fire in a charcoal grill, or preheat a gas grill to medium-high.

To prepare the poached tomatoes, place a saucepan over medium-low heat and pour in the garlic confit oil. Carefully place the heirloom tomatoes in the oil and slowly warm them. Stir gently and frequently, being careful not to break them open. The goal here is to just heat them through,

letting some of the oil permeate their flesh; do not boil the tomatoes in the oil.

Remove from the heat and carefully transfer the tomatoes and oil into a colander set over a small bowl. Strain off the oil and reserve both the tomatoes and the oil in a warm place.

To prepare the salmon, season the salmon pieces with salt and rub canola oil all over them. Make sure your grill is well coated with oil, and have ready a thin metal spatula that is as large as your fish fillets for turning the salmon.

Grill the salmon pieces on both sides for about 5 minutes per side, or until they are medium rare. Fresh king salmon is best served slightly rare.

To serve, in 4 shallow bowls or on dinner plates with rimmed edges, create a bed of the warm tomatoes, interplaying the colors, and sprinkle with a little fleur de sel. Rest a piece of salmon on each bed of tomatoes, top with a dollop of the tomato mousse, and garnish with the micro greens. Serve immediately, with a little dish of the warm tomato poaching oil.

Hawaiian Swordfish with Tarragon, Gnocchi, and Vegetable Émincée with a Vermouth Butter Sauce

Serves 4

I love the texture of swordfish. Its meaty consistency allows for a lot of diversity in cooking: it is phenomenal grilled and even has enough natural oil for poaching. We acquire our swordfish known as Shutome´, from Hawaii, where there is abundance, and the quality is always excellent. Many people are concerned with the depletion of this fish, as are we, and the care taken in fishing these waters is commendable. For this recipe, I cut the swordfish into small, thin medallions. This way, they cook through yet remain moist. You will want a gnocchi board (see page 221) to create the classic ridges on the gnocchi, which hold the sauce.

GNOCCHI

2 pounds baking potatoes, about 3 large russets

Canola oil, for coating potatoes

1¹/₂ teaspoons salt, plus more for sprinkling on potatoes

2 egg yolks

1 egg

1¹/₂ cups all-purpose flour

VERMOUTH BUTTER SAUCE

¹/₂ cup dry vermouth

¹/₂ cup white wine vinegar

¹/₄ cup rice vinegar

2 tablespoons freshly squeezed lemon juice

1 shallot, sliced

6 black peppercorns

1 bay leaf

1 sprig thyme

1¹/₂ cups unsalted butter, cut into 1-inch cubes and refrigerated

Kosher salt

Freshly ground white pepper

VEGETABLE ÉMINCÉE

6 cups water

3 tablespoons kosher salt, plus more to taste

12 asparagus tips, 3 inches long

8 baby carrots, thinly sliced on the diagonal

1 tablespoon unsalted butter

1 shallot, finely diced

Kosher salt

Freshly ground white pepper

1 tablespoon chopped fresh tarragon

1 to 2 pounds trimmed loin of swordfish, 6 to 8 inches in length, 3 inches in diameter

Kosher salt

Freshly ground white pepper

Canola oil, for rubbing on fish

4 sprigs of fresh tarragon, for garnish

Zest of 1 lemon, for garnish

Preheat the oven to 375°F.

To prepare the gnocchi, scrub the potatoes under cold running water, and dry them well. Place the potatoes on a baking sheet, coat them with oil, and salt them liberally. Place in the center of the oven and bake for 1 hour, or until fork-tender. Remove from the oven. Let cool for 10 minutes. While the potatoes are still hot, peel them and press them through a potato ricer into a nonreactive bowl.

Make a well in the potatoes and add the salt, egg yolks, and whole egg. Using a wooden spoon, gently mix. Add the flour, a little at a time, and with your hands, lightly stir the mixture with a cutting motion, just until it forms a ball of dough. Try not to

overmix, or your gnocchi will tend to get heavy. Sprinkle flour onto a clean, even surface. Transfer the gnocchi dough onto the flour and gently knead the dough for a minute or so, until smooth. It may become necessary to add a bit more flour to prevent the dough from sticking to the surface.

Line a baking pan with floured parchment.

Divide the dough into 3 pieces. Roll each piece into a ropelike shape, the thickness of a roll of pennies. Cut into about $1^1/2$-inch slices, and roll them out on a floured gnocchi board. Roll them directly into the baking pan. Continue the process until all the dough is used. Cover and refrigerate.

To prepare the sauce, place a saucepan over medium heat and add the vermouth, white wine vinegar, rice vinegar, lemon juice, shallot, peppercorns, bay leaf, and thyme. Cook for 10 minutes, until about 2 tablespoons of liquid remain in the pan. Remove from the heat and, with a wooden spoon, stir in 4 cubes of the chilled butter, until thoroughly incorporated.

Place the pan over low heat and stir in the remaining butter, a cube at a time, until thoroughly incorporated. Remove from the heat immediately, and strain through a chinois into a bowl. Season to taste with salt and white pepper. Set aside in a warm but not hot place, as too much heat will cause the emulsified sauce to separate.

To boil the gnocchi, bring a large pot of salted water to a boil. Add the desired number of gnocchi, and boil for about 5 minutes, until they rise to the surface. Continue to cook for 1 minute, until cooked through. Remove from the heat and, using a slotted spoon, transfer to a bowl.

To prepare the émincée, place 4 cups of water and 2 tablespoons salt in one saucepan and 2 cups of water and 1 tablespoon salt in another saucepan. Bring both to a boil over medium-high heat. Fill 2 bowls with ice water. Blanch the asparagus in the 4 cups boiling water for about 2 minutes, until al dente. Using a slotted spoon or strainer, transfer to one of the ice water baths. Shock for about 1 minute, until thoroughly chilled. Immediately transfer to a colander and drain.

Blanch the carrots in the 2 cups boiling water for 4 minutes, until al dente. Using a slotted spoon or strainer, transfer to the other ice water bath. Shock for about 1 minute, until thoroughly chilled. Immediately transfer to a colander and drain.

Place a sauté pan over medium-high heat, and add the butter. When the butter begins bubbling, add the shallot, asparagus, carrots, and salt and white pepper to taste. Sauté for 2 minutes, until heated through. Add the cooked gnocchi and the tarragon, and stir gently to combine. Remove from the heat, and set in a warm place.

To prepare the swordfish, cut the loin of swordfish into 8 medallions, $3/4$ inch thick. Dry the flesh with a paper towel, season with salt and white pepper, and rub the fish with canola oil.

Place a heavy-bottomed skillet over high heat. When the pan is hot, sear each medallion for about 2 minutes per side, until cooked through.

To assemble, divide the gnocchi and vegetables among 4 shallow bowls, and stack 2 pieces of the swordfish over them, one on top of another. Spoon the sauce around the base of the stacks and over the top of the fish. Garnish with the tarragon and lemon zest. Serve immediately.

Prosciutto-Wrapped Monkfish with Sea Clams, Baby Bok Choy, and a Burgundy Sauce

Serves 4

Monkfish is really a unique fish. It can reach up to one hundred pounds in weight, and its head is huge in proportion to its body; the mouth can sometimes reach a foot across. Known as an anglerfish, the monkfish has its own little fishing pole. The spine ends in a flexible, extensible cord that dangles in front of its mouth, serving as a fishing lure for catching prey. If you can't picture this, imagine an ugly bulldog with fins and a single antenna!

The edible portion, the flesh from its muscular tail, is dense, sweet, and most desirable to use for almost any cooking method: sautéing, broiling, poaching, and so forth. I have heard many people say that it tastes just like lobster. To me, that's a stretch, but it's true that monkfish will work beautifully in any recipe where you might use lobster meat. As with all fish, be sure to buy the freshest monkfish you can find.

8 ounces sliced fresh clam meat

1/2 cup chopped fresh basil

1 tablespoon minced shallot

Pinch of freshly ground white pepper

4 pieces of cleaned monkfish fillet, 6 ounces each

8 thin slices Italian prosciutto

1/2 cup water

2 tablespoons kosher salt

4 heads baby bok choy

BURGUNDY SAUCE

2 tablespoons unsalted butter

1 tablespoon minced shallot

1/2 teaspoon minced garlic

1 sprig fresh thyme

1 bay leaf

6 black peppercorns

1 cup Burgundy wine

1 cup veal stock (page 216)

1 tablespoon unsalted butter

2 tablespoons unsalted butter

2 tablespoons light olive oil

Kosher salt

Freshly ground white pepper

Basil oil (page 204), for garnish

Lightly oil a baking dish large enough to hold the fish pieces.

To prepare the monkfish, in a small bowl, combine the clam meat, basil, shallot, and white pepper. Divide into 4 portions. Place a mound of the seasoned clam meat on top of each of the fish fillets, pack down, and wrap a thin slice of the prosciutto around the whole fillet. Lay the other slice of prosciutto across the first one and wrap it to firmly secure the clam filling. Place in the baking dish, cover, and refrigerate.

To blanch the bok choy, pour the water into a saucepan and add the salt. Bring to a boil over high heat. Fill a bowl with ice water. Blanch the bok choy in the boiling water for about 2 minutes. Using a slotted spoon or strainer, transfer the bok choy to the ice water bath. Shock for about 1 minute, until thoroughly chilled. Immediately transfer to a colander and drain.

To prepare the sauce, place a small saucepan over medium heat, and add the butter. When the butter has melted, add the shallot, garlic, thyme, bay

leaf, and peppercorns. Cook for 2 minutes, until the shallot and garlic start to sweat. Add the Burgundy and cook for 5 minutes, until the liquid is reduced by half. Pour in the veal stock and decrease the heat to low. Simmer for 15 minutes, until the sauce is reduced to about $1/2$ cup. Strain through a fine chinois into a ceramic bowl. Stir in the remaining butter. Set in a warm place.

Preheat the oven to 350°F.

To bake the monkfish, remove the fish from the refrigerator and place in the oven. Bake for 15 minutes, until quite firm. Monkfish needs to be cooked thoroughly. The prosciutto will contract and tighten up, making the fish easier to handle.

Warm 4 dinner plates.

To prepare the bok choy, place a sauté pan over medium heat and add the butter. When the butter has melted, add the olive oil, and lay the bok choy in the pan, cut sides down. Season with salt and white pepper. Decrease the heat to low and cook, covered, for 2 minutes, until heated through. Remove from the heat. The bok choy should be hot but still crisp.

To serve, place a bed of the bok choy on each plate, and set a piece of the fish atop it. Puddle a little sauce on the plate. Place a few drops of the basil oil around the fish. Serve immediately.

Lemon "Larded" Sea Bass with English Cucumber and Parsley Coulis and Osetra Caviar

Serves 4

The term *larded* in this recipe is actually a play on words. Larding is the act of inserting strips of fat into meat, with what is essentially a sort of large sewing needle called a larding needle. This is done to very lean pieces of meat, to add flavor and moisture. In this recipe, we infuse the fish with Meyer lemon zest in the same fashion, and its sole purpose is to flavor the fish with a strong lemon essence. The cucumber and parsley coulis is very mild and is an excellent contrast to the strong flavors of the salty caviar, and the bright, tart lemon.

I blanch the lemon zest twice, salt and sugar it, cover it with extra virgin olive oil, and marinate it for a week. This produces a really tender, succulent lemon zest that nearly dissolves in the flesh of the fish, creating a luscious pungency that just screams of lemon. You can go ahead and just use fresh lemon zest. However, if you take the time to prepare the Meyer lemon zest as we do, you'll find that the results are worth it.

LEMON CONFIT

Zest of 6 Meyer lemons

1 teaspoon fleur de sel

1 tablespoon superfine sugar

1 teaspoon minced shallot

1 cup extra virgin olive oil

4 sea bass fillets, 2 inches thick, about 2 pounds

ENGLISH CUCUMBER AND PARSLEY COULIS

4 cups water

1 tablespoon kosher salt

1/2 cup Italian parsley leaves

2 peeled and seeded English cucumbers

2 tablespoons sour cream

1 teaspoon rice vinegar

Kosher salt

Kosher salt

Freshly ground white pepper

Canola oil, for searing fish

12 lengthwise slices of washed English cucumber, each 6 inches long and 1/8 inch thick

12 peeled, seeded slices of Meyer lemon

2 ounces osetra caviar

2 baby artichoke hearts, quartered, for garnish

4 sprigs dill, for garnish

Set out a bowl of ice water, a plate with several layers of paper towels, and a 2-cup glass or plastic storage container.

To prepare the lemon confit, fill 2 small saucepans with water, place over high heat, and bring to a boil. Drop the lemon zest into the first pan of boiling water, and cook for 1 minute, until soft. Using a slotted spoon, transfer the zest into the second pan of boiling water. Cook for 1 more minute. Using a slotted spoon, transfer the zest into the ice water and shock it for 10 seconds. Transfer to the paper towels to dry. Place the lemon zest in the storage container, and stir in the salt, sugar, and shallot. Pour in the olive oil to cover. Seal and refrigerate for 1 week, or up to a month.

When you are ready to use the marinated lemon zest, set a small colander over a bowl. Let the marinated lemon come to room temperature, and drain it through the colander until most of the oil is drained off. Reserve the oil.

Using a knife with a sharp point, make 5 incisions, $1/2$ inch deep, into the flesh of the fish. Using a pair of kitchen tweezers, grasp a small amount of the lemon zest, and push it into the incisions in the fish. Fill all the holes with the lemon zest. Transfer the fish to a plate, cover, and refrigerate.

To blanch the parsley, pour the water into a saucepan and add the salt. Bring to a boil over medium-high heat. Fill a bowl with ice water. Blanch the parsley in the boiling water for 15 seconds. Using a slotted spoon or strainer, transfer the leaves to the ice water bath. Shock for about 1 minute, or until thoroughly chilled. Immediately transfer to a colander and drain. Press out all the water.

Preheat the oven to 400°F.

To prepare the coulis, place the peeled and seeded cucumbers, parsley, sour cream, rice vinegar, and salt to taste into a blender, and purée until smooth.

Remove the sea bass from the refrigerator and season with salt and white pepper. Place a heavy-bottomed, ovenproof sauté pan over medium-high heat and pour in a thin layer of oil. When the oil is hot, sear the fish, turning once, for 2 minutes per side, until golden in color. Drain the excess oil out of the pan, and place the pan in the oven for 10 minutes, or until the fish is firm to the touch. Remove from the oven.

To serve, set out 4 dinner plates, and on each place 3 lengths of the sliced cucumber, with 3 slices of the Meyer lemon. Spoon some of the coulis into the center of each plate, and set a fish fillet atop. Spoon $1/2$-ounce of caviar onto each piece of fish, and garnish with the artichoke hearts and dill. Serve immediately.

Hawaiian Tuna with "Hot" Shrimp Risotto and Carrot and English Pea Salad

Serves 4

Tori is my Honolulu fish connection, and one of the most passionate fishmongers I have ever met. She not only sells ultra-pristine tuna, shiny, ruby red, translucent, and beautiful, but also knows why they are that way, who caught them, where they were running, and why a certain fish needs to be on my menu tomorrow. Living in the desert, we need to receive fresh tuna by air—no three-days-on-a-truck fish is served in our kitchen. Cooking a piece of sushi-grade fish any more than rare to medium rare is truly doing this gift of the sea an injustice. Tuna has a distinctly rich-flavored flesh that is moderate to high in fat, firmly textured, and tender. Fresh tuna is similar to a lean piece of meat, like a tenderloin of beef, that is tender and juicy when rare but becomes dry and loses its flavorful juices if overcooked. My advice is to buy it really fresh, and eat it rare.

"HOT" SHRIMP RISOTTO

2 tablespoons extra virgin olive oil

2 shallots, finely diced

1 cup Carnaroli rice

$^1/_2$ cup dry white wine

$2^1/_2$ cups shrimp stock (page 216)

2 serrano peppers, stems removed and thinly sliced

2 cups cleaned, diced raw shrimp

2 tablespoons hot chile sauce

2 tablespoons unsalted butter

$^1/_4$ cup grated Parmigiano-Reggiano cheese

2 tablespoons heavy cream, whipped to soft peaks

CARROT AND ENGLISH PEA SALAD

6 cups water

2 teaspoons kosher salt

$^1/_4$ cup sliced baby carrots

$^1/_2$ cup shelled fresh English peas

2 tablespoons light olive oil

1 teaspoon toasted sesame oil

1 teaspoon rice vinegar

1 teaspoon honey

Kosher salt

2 cups frisée lettuce, white part only

$^1/_2$ cup pea sprouts

4 sushi-grade ahi tuna steaks, 1 inch thick

Fleur de sel

Peanut oil, untoasted, for rubbing on fish

4 teaspoons hot chile sauce, for garnish

To prepare the risotto, place a large, heavy-bottomed skillet over medium-low heat, and add the oil. When the oil is hot, add the shallots and cook for 1 minute, until they are translucent. Pour in the rice, stir to coat with the oil, and cook for about 3 minutes, until the rice forms a light crust. Add the wine slowly and cook for 5 minutes, stirring frequently with a wooden spoon, until it is absorbed.

Add 1 cup of the shrimp stock and cook for about 3 minutes, stirring frequently, until all the liquid is absorbed. Continue adding the rest of the stock slowly, as the rice soaks up the liquid, cooking for 12 to 15 more minutes, until most of the stock is absorbed.

Add the serrano peppers, shrimp, and chile sauce, and cook for about 3 minutes, stirring frequently, until the shrimp are just barely done. Add the butter, cheese, and heavy cream. Stir gently just to combine. Remove from the heat and keep warm.

The consistency of the rice should be soft at first and end with a chewy texture. The more often you make and eat risotto, the more you will know what it's supposed to be like and what texture appeals to you.

To prepare the salad, place 2 cups of water and 1 teaspoon salt in one saucepan and 4 cups of water and 1 teaspoon salt in another saucepan. Bring both to a boil over high heat. Fill 2 bowls with ice water. Blanch the carrots in the 2 cups boiling water for about 2 minutes, until al dente. Using a slotted spoon or strainer, transfer to one of the ice water baths. Shock for about 1 minute, until thoroughly chilled. Immediately transfer to a colander and drain.

Blanch the peas in the 4 cups boiling water for about 2 minutes. Using a slotted spoon or strainer, transfer to the other ice water bath. Shock for about 1 minute, until thoroughly chilled. Immediately transfer to a colander and drain.

Place the olive oil, sesame oil, rice vinegar, honey, and kosher salt to taste in a metal bowl and whisk together. Add the frisée, blanched carrots and peas, and pea sprouts. Toss gently until all the leaves are coated.

To sear the tuna, preheat a heavy-bottomed or cast iron skillet over high heat. Prepare a smooth surface for cutting the finished tuna steaks. Warm 4 dinner plates.

Season the tuna steaks with fleur de sel, and rub with peanut oil. When the pan is very hot, sear the tuna on each side for about 30 seconds. Remove from the heat immediately.

To serve, cut the tuna steaks into 3 triangles. Spoon some of the hot risotto into the center of each of the dinner plates, and on each place a small stack of the 3 tuna triangles. Arrange the salad over the tuna, and dollop 1 teaspoon of chile sauce at the edge of the risotto. Serve immediately.

Fiery Chile Prawns with Crispy Jasmine Almond Rice Cakes and Caper Basil Sauce

Serves 4

Living in the land of chile, most all of us become passionate aficionados, in constant longing for this staple of our local cuisine. Northern New Mexico natives and recent imports alike ritually roast, peel, and seed tons of these hot chiles every fall and, as they say here, "put them up," which actually means, store them in the freezer for winter use. Hatch, New Mexico, is the spot where most of our very picante green chiles come from, with their burn and roar and also a mysterious, aromatic sweetness. The basting sauce I make for this dish is sort of a sambal, which is an Indonesian table condiment of uncooked chile, garlic, and spices. A favorite on our menu, this dish is not for the capsicum fearfuls! It truly is *hot*, if you're using the chiles I recommend. It is designed to please those who come in wanting the dose of chile they came to New Mexico to eat. Of course, you may substitute a milder variety more to your liking.

You will need a deep-fat fryer to make the rice cakes.

JASMINE ALMOND RICE CAKES

2 tablespoons light olive oil

$1/4$ cup minced yellow onion

$1^1/2$ cups jasmine rice

$1^1/4$ cups water

$3/4$ cup almond milk (page 202)

1 cup slivered almonds, toasted (page 219)

2 tablespoons minced green onion

1 teaspoon kosher salt

Cornstarch, for dredging

CHILE SAUCE

6 fresh hot pasilla or cascabel chiles

2 sprigs cilantro

2 sun-dried tomatoes, rehydrated

1 clove garlic

1 tablespoon apple cider vinegar

$1/2$ teaspoon shrimp paste

1 tablespoon extra virgin olive oil

$1/2$ teaspoon kosher salt

$1/2$ cup honey

4 cups water

1 tablespoon salt

1 cup basil leaves

CAPER BASIL SAUCE

1 tablespoon minced fresh Italian parsley

$1/2$ teaspoon minced garlic

3 tablespoons freshly squeezed lemon juice

$1/2$ cup water

2 tablespoons small nonpareil capers

1 cup aïoli (page 202)

Kosher salt

4 cups peanut oil, for deep-frying

16 jumbo prawns, cleaned and deveined, tails left on

Sea salt

Freshly ground white pepper

Peanut oil, for coating prawns

SALAD

1 cup mâche

16 fresh basil leaves

Dash of freshly squeezed lemon juice

Kosher salt

To prepare the rice cakes, place a heavy-bottomed saucepan over medium heat and add the olive oil. When the oil is hot, sauté the onion for about

3 minutes, until it is translucent. Add the rice and stir to coat. Add the water, almond milk, toasted almonds, green onion, and salt. Stir once, and bring to a boil. Decrease the heat to low, and allow to simmer, covered, without stirring, for 20 to 25 minutes, or until all the liquid is absorbed and the rice is tender.

In a buttered baking pan, spread out the rice mixture to a thickness of about $1/2$ inch. Cover with a sheet of plastic wrap and refrigerate for at least 2 hours before cutting. Using a 2-inch round cookie cutter, cut out 8 circles of rice cake and dredge them in cornstarch. Transfer to a plate, cover, and refrigerate.

To prepare the chile sauce, remove the stems of the chiles and cut in half. Place the chiles in a large blender. Add the cilantro, sun-dried tomato, garlic, vinegar, shrimp paste, olive oil, and salt. Purée until smooth. Add the honey, and pulse for 1 minute. Transfer to a small bowl.

To blanch the basil, pour the water into a saucepan and add the salt. Bring to a boil over medium-high heat. Fill a bowl with ice water. Blanch the basil in the boiling water for 15 seconds. Using a slotted spoon or strainer, transfer the leaves to the ice water bath. Shock for about 1 minute, until thoroughly chilled. Immediately transfer to a colander and drain. Press out all the water.

To prepare the caper basil sauce, place the basil, parsley, garlic, lemon juice, and water in a blender, and mix until smooth. Transfer the mixture to a bowl and fold in the capers and aïoli. Add salt if needed. Cover and refrigerate until ready to serve.

Prepare a medium-hot fire on one side of a charcoal grill, or preheat one side of a gas grill to medium-high.

Preheat the oil in a deep-fat fryer to 350°F.

To grill the prawns, season the prawns with salt and pepper and coat them with oil. Make sure your grill is well oiled to prevent the prawns from sticking. On the hottest part of the grill, cook the prawns for about 1 minute on each side, until the flesh has marks from the grill. Liberally brush them with the chile sauce. Move them to the side of the grill where the heat is lower; the sugar in the sauce will cause the prawns to burn if left over too hot a fire. Brush again liberally with the chile sauce.

Continue to cook for about 2 minutes, just until firm, and set aside. Be careful not to overcook the prawns, or they will become rubbery.

Prepare a plate with several layers of paper towels.

Fry the rice cakes in the deep-fat fryer for 2 minutes, until golden brown. Using a slotted spoon or a spider, remove the rice cakes and transfer them directly to the paper towels to drain.

To prepare the salad, in a small bowl, mix the mâche and basil leaves together and toss with the lemon and salt. On each of 4 dinner plates, layer the rice cakes and the prawns. Spoon some of the caper basil sauce around the bottom rice cake. Place the salad on top, for garnish. Serve immediately.

Grilled Coldwater Lobster Tails and Creamy Chili Vinaigrette with Savory Potato Cakes

Serves 4

I dare not venture to guess how many lobsters we have served here at Geronimo. One of the reasons is this popular dish. From the cold waters off the coast of Maine come these beautiful, sweet crustaceans. Flavored by rich cherrywood smoke from the grill, sauced in the garlicky tang of the spicy, creamy vinaigrette, and combined with crunchy potato cakes, this dish just hums.

CREAMY CHILI VINAIGRETTE

1 cup fresh mayonnaise (page 209)

$1/4$ cup chopped cilantro

3 tablespoons red wine vinegar

2 tablespoons freshly squeezed lemon juice

2 tablespoons Vietnamese chili sauce

1 teaspoon or more minced garlic

2 teaspoons honey

14 tablespoons ($3/4$ cup plus 2 tablespoons) light olive oil

POTATO CAKES

1 pound baking potatoes, about 2 medium russets

2 tablespoons very finely diced chives

$1/2$ cup thinly sliced shallot

1 tablespoon kosher salt

$1/2$ teaspoon freshly ground black pepper

Light olive oil, for sautéing

COMPOTE

1 tablespoon unsalted butter

2 tablespoons sliced shallot

1 cup fresh sweet corn kernels, cut from about 2 ears

$1/2$ cup cabbage chiffonade

2 tablespoons capers

Pinch of salt

Pinch of freshly ground white pepper

8 coldwater lobster tails, 4 ounces each, split and deveined

$1/4$ cup canola oil

Kosher salt

Freshly ground white pepper

Opal basil leaves, for garnish

Celery leaves, for garnish

Basil aïoli (page 204), for garnish (optional)

Vietnamese chili sauce, for garnish (optional)

To prepare the vinaigrette, combine the mayonnaise, cilantro, vinegar, lemon juice, Vietnamese chili sauce, garlic, honey, and light olive oil in a bowl. Whisk until thoroughly incorporated. Cover and refrigerate until ready to serve.

Prepare a plate with several layers of paper towels.

To prepare the potato cakes, wash the potatoes, peel, and place in a bowl of water. Immediately before cooking the cakes, place the julienne cutter side of a mandoline over a bowl, and shred the potatoes into the bowl. Add the chives, shallot, salt, and pepper. Using a wooden spoon, mix gently and well. Place a large, nonstick sauté pan over medium heat. Divide the potato mixture equally into 8 cakes. Pour a thin coating of oil into the pan. Brown the potato cakes for 3 minutes per side, turning once, until both sides are crisp. Using a spider or spatula, transfer the cakes onto the paper towel and drain. Set aside in a warm place.

Prepare a medium-hot fire in a charcoal grill, or preheat a gas grill to medium-high.

To prepare the compote, place a sauté pan over medium heat and add the butter. When the butter has melted, add the shallot, corn, cabbage, and capers. Sauté for about 2 minutes, until slightly

wilted. Remove from the heat. Season with the salt and white pepper.

To grill the lobster tails, place all the tails in a bowl, add the oil, and toss until fully coated. Season with salt and white pepper. Place on the well-oiled grill, flesh side down, for 2 minutes, or until cooked almost through. Turn each half tail and place, shell side down, on the cooler side of the grill. Do not turn the lobster tails over again, because valuable juice forms in the shell of the lobster.

To assemble, place a mound of the compote in the center of each of 4 dinner plates, surrounded by dollops of the vinaigrette. Stack 4 lobster half tails, one on top of the other, on the cabbage mixture

and top with 2 of the crispy potato cakes. Garnish with the basil and tender celery leaves. For a spicier dish, surround the lobster tails with droplets of the Vietnamese chili sauce and the basil aïoli. Serve immediately.

Leek-Wrapped Sea Scallops with Lobster Oil and Black Lentil Risotto

Serves 4

Buying scallops isn't what it used to be. Scallop buyers today need a whole new vocabulary, including "chemical free," "dry pack," and "day boat." We use only dry-pack or day boat scallops, as do most fine restaurants, because they are truly fresh: usually shucked right there on the boat, then dry-packed, and next-day-aired to us, on a speeding jet. Their flesh is opalescent and shiny, and they are firm and succulent. They cook like a lean steak, and eat like the finest thing you've ever put in your mouth. When you sear these, they caramelize and get a sweet, crisp skin. Once you have cooked a dry-pack scallop, you will never go back to the brine-packed ones.

For this recipe, I enfold the scallops in a leek ribbon to infuse the leek flavor into their flesh. Wrapping the scallops into a tight, cylindrical shape also helps hold in the valuable juices. Buy U8 scallops, which are 8 or fewer to the pound. You will need wooden or metal skewers and raw lobster shells, often available in the fish department at your local grocer. The lentils in the risotto recipe need to be soaked in cold water overnight.

LOBSTER OIL

3 cups canola oil

1 pound smashed uncooked lobster shells, about 4 cups

$^1/_4$ cup vermouth

$^1/_4$ cup rice vinegar

2 cloves garlic, split

2 tablespoons chopped white onion

2 tablespoons chopped peeled carrot

1 tablespoon crustacean spice (page 206)

4 cups water

1 tablespoon kosher salt

8 leek ribbons, each 6 by $1^1/_2$ inches

8 large, dry-pack scallops

BLACK LENTIL RISOTTO

$^1/_2$ cup black beluga lentils, soaked overnight

2 tablespoons extra virgin olive oil

2 shallots, finely diced

1 tablespoon finely diced applewood-smoked bacon

1 cup Carnaroli rice

1 cup dry white wine

$1^1/_2$ cups blonde chicken stock (page 213)

1 tablespoon very finely diced peeled carrot

1 tablespoon very finely diced celery hearts

1 tablespoon very finely diced leek, white part only

2 tablespoons unsalted butter

$^1/_4$ cup grated Parmigiano-Reggiano cheese

2 tablespoons heavy cream, whipped to soft peaks

Kosher salt

Freshly ground white pepper

Canola oil, for oiling scallops

Mint sprigs, for garnish

Preheat the oven to 350°F.

To prepare the lobster oil, place a Dutch oven over high heat and add $^1/_2$ cup of the oil. When the oil is hot, about 200°F, add the lobster shells and cook for 10 minutes, stirring frequently, until they turn bright red. Decrease the heat to medium, and deglaze the shells with the vermouth and vinegar. Cook for 2 minutes, stirring frequently, until the

liquid evaporates. Add the garlic, onion, carrot, and crustacean spice. Stir and add the remaining 2^1/$_2$ cups oil. Place the Dutch oven in the preheated oven. Cook for 45 minutes, until the flavor has infused into the oil. Remove from the oven and let cool for 30 minutes.

Fit a chinois into a tall-sided, deep bowl with a well-balanced, flat bottom. Place a large coffee filter, or multiple layers of cheesecloth, inside the chinois. Strain the shells, turning them once or twice, making sure all the valuable oils drain off. Transfer the oil into a squeeze bottle.

To blanch the leek ribbons, pour the water into a saucepan, add the salt, and bring to a boil over medium-high heat. Fill a bowl with ice water. Blanch the leek ribbons in the boiling water for 15 seconds. Using a slotted spoon or strainer, transfer to the ice water bath. Shock for about 1 minute, or until thoroughly chilled. Immediately transfer the leek ribbons to a colander and drain. Press out all the water.

Wrap a leek ribbon around the circumference of a scallop. Push a skewer all the way through the scallop to the other side, to secure the leek. Repeat this step with the remaining 7 scallops. Transfer to a plate. Cover and refrigerate until ready to cook.

For the risotto, place a pot of salted water over medium-high heat and bring to a boil. Transfer the lentils to a colander, rinse well under cold running water, and drain. Add the lentils to the boiling water and cook for about 20 minutes, until tender. Remove from the heat. Drain in a colander.

Place a large skillet or heavy-bottomed sauté pan over medium heat, and pour in the oil. When the oil is hot, add the shallot and bacon. Cook for about 5 minutes, until the shallot is translucent. Pour in the rice, stir to coat with oil, and cook the rice for about 3 minutes, until it forms a light crust. Add the white wine slowly and cook for 2 minutes, stirring frequently with a wooden spoon, until the it is absorbed. Add 1 cup of the chicken stock and the carrot, celery, and leek, and cook for 5 minutes, stirring frequently, until the liquid is absorbed. Continue adding the rest of the stock, a little at a time, as the rice soaks up the liquid, cooking for 12 to 15 minutes, until most of the stock is absorbed.

Gently fold in the lentils, butter, cheese, whipped cream, and any remaining stock. Remove from the heat and keep warm. The consistency of the rice should be soft at first and end with a slightly chewy texture.

Warm 4 dinner plates.

To cook the scallops, place a cast iron Griswold or heavy-bottomed skillet over high heat. Season the exposed surfaces of the scallops with salt, white pepper, and canola oil. Sear the scallops for 1 minute on each side, until crusted brown. Remove from the heat. Let the scallops remain in the hot pan. For optimum flavor, the scallops should be somewhat rare inside. If you choose to cook them all the way through, sear them for 1 more minute on each side, being careful not to burn them.

To serve, spoon a mound of the risotto on each of the 4 warm plates. Remove the skewers from the scallops and place 2 atop each mound of risotto. Drizzle the lobster oil over and around the scallops and risotto. Garnish with mint sprigs, and serve immediately.

Mexican Beer-Battered Soft-Shell Crabs with Farm-fresh Organic Egg, Fingerling Potato, Cabbage, and Cornichon Salad with Malt and Balsamic Vinegar Syrup

Serves 4

Soft-shell crabs! What a perfect way to celebrate the coming of summer. During their season, they are a must on our menu. I have eaten many a fried fish, crustacean, and mollusk, but nothing, nothing, compares to the love I have for a soft shell crab. When I lived near Baltimore, Maryland, home of the famous Inner Harbor, my friends and I used to head down to the market place to visit the "Crabman," as we called him. This little old man, with his rubber fishing outfit, was there every time we came. He'd be cleaning crabs by the bucketful, while his little apprentice rolled them in flour, and dropped them for a minute or two, in a vat of bubbling, hot oil. Fried up, the crabs were handed off to the next guy, who would prepare the sandwich: big, thick slices of Wonder bread, homemade tartar sauce, a huge slab of iceberg lettuce, and a giant tomato slice. "Coleslaw or potato salad?" they would shout, "Next!" The sandwiches were great, and being a passionate crab lover, I had to add a few shakes of malt vinegar. We ate as many as we could, with dank Clipper City Pale Ale. This recipe also displays my love for vinegar, egg, and potato salad. The salad can be made ahead of time, which improves the flavor, and then the dish is quite simple to assemble.

It is very important to purchase crabs that are alive. I recommend, if you're squeamish, that you have your fishmonger clean the crabs for this recipe, because you actually need to cut off their faces with sharp scissors while they are, dare I say it, still alive. Also, the lungs need to be removed, and the point trimmed off the shell. You will need a deep-fat fryer to fry the crabs.

EGG AND POTATO SALAD

1/2 cup fresh mayonnaise (see page 209)

2 tablespoons minced chives

2 tablespoons minced shallot

1/2 cup shredded cabbage

1/4 cup diced cornichon

1/4 cup finely diced celery hearts

8 fingerling potatoes, cooked and sliced

3 hard-boiled, diced Taos eggs or other farm-fresh eggs

Kosher salt

Freshly ground white pepper

VINEGAR SYRUPS

1 cup balsamic vinegar

1 1/2 cups malt vinegar

1 teaspoon light corn syrup

BEER-BATTERED CRABS

Peanut oil, for deep-frying

2 1/2 cups all-purpose flour

2 tablespoons light olive oil

2 eggs, separated

3/4 teaspoon salt

1/2 teaspoon minced garlic

2 cups cold Negra Modelo or other dark beer

8 cleaned soft-shell blue crabs

WATERCRESS SALAD

1 bunch baby watercress, washed and trimmed

1 tablespoon coarsely chopped fresh dill

12 chive sticks, 2 inches long

Grated zest of 1 lemon

Dash of malt vinegar

Kosher salt

To prepare the potato salad, place the mayonnaise, chives, shallot, cabbage, cornichon, and celery in a chilled bowl and mix until incorporated. Gently fold in the potatoes and the eggs. Season to taste with salt and white pepper. Cover and refrigerate until ready to serve.

To prepare the syrups, place a small saucepan over medium-low heat, add the balsamic vinegar, and cook for about 10 minutes, until reduced to about 2 syrupy tablespoons. Place a second small saucepan over medium-low heat, add the malt vinegar and corn syrup, and cook for about 10 minutes, until reduced to about 2 syrupy tablespoons. Set the two syrups aside.

To prepare the crabs, pour the peanut oil in a deep-fat fryer, and preheat it to 350°F.

Place the flour, olive oil, egg yolks, salt, garlic, and beer in a bowl. Set the bowl over an ice water bath, and whisk the mixture just until smooth; do not overmix. In a clean metal bowl, whisk the egg whites into soft peaks, and fold into the chilled batter.

Prepare a plate with several layers of paper towels.

Very gently, being careful not to break the legs off, dip the crabs into the batter, and let the excess batter drain off. Drop the crabs 2 at a time into the fryer, and cook for about 2 minutes, until golden brown. Using a slotted spoon or spider, transfer the crabs to the paper towels and drain.

To prepare the salad, toss the watercress, dill, chives, lemon zest, vinegar, and salt in a small salad bowl.

In the center of each of 4 dinner plates, mound a generous portion of potato salad. Set 2 crabs atop each portion, and finish with a sprinkling of the watercress salad. Drizzle the vinegar syrups around and over the crabs and potato salad. Serve immediately.

"Big Bowl" of Washington State Mussels, Manila Clams, and Scallops, with Meyer Lemon and Fennel

Serves 4

I love to make this simple recipe for a table of friends who will dig in and share a big bowl of mollusks before their dinner. I use three different kinds—mussels, scallops, and clams—and I make sure that they are all nearly the same size, so that they will open at approximately the same time during cooking. Always scrub the mollusks before cooking, to remove any sand or grown-on algae. This is especially true for the mussels, because they anchor themselves to rocks, pilings, and other mussels with their "byssal threads," or "beard." This anchoring allows the mussels to remain fixed in one location. You will need to pull the byssal threads off before cooking. Do this as close to cooking time as possible. If shellfish don't readily close when lightly tapped, it's best not to buy them.

This recipe can be easily doubled, and so forth. If I have a lot of people over for dinner, I will build a fire outside, set a large rondeau directly on the flames, and cook up 12 pounds. The scrumptious accompanying sauce just begs for a dunkable bread to go with it. I love to serve lots of "grill bread." Basically, it's uncooked, risen bread dough that's been rolled in olive oil, garlic, and salt. I tear off pieces, form them into flat oblongs, and toss them on the grill to cook. For this recipe you will need a large rondeau or other large, deep pot with a lid.

1/2 cup light olive oil

2 baby fennel bulbs, cut in half, cores removed, and layers separated

1 bouquet garni (page 205)

1/2 cup minced fresh garlic

3 tablespoons freshly ground black pepper

Freshly squeezed juice of 4 Meyer lemons

1/2 cup Pernod

4 cups dry white wine

2 cups lobster stock (page 215)

2 pounds mussels, cleaned and bearded

2 pounds scallops in the shell, cleaned

2 pounds Manila clams, cleaned

Fennel fronds, for garnish

Set out a large serving bowl.

Place a large rondeau over high heat, and pour in the olive oil. When the oil is hot, add the fennel, bouquet garni, garlic, and pepper. Sauté for 2 minutes, until the garlic starts to brown slightly. Add the lemon juice, Pernod, white wine, and lobster stock. Bring the liquid to a boil and add the mollusks. Stir with a thick, strong wooden spoon to coat the mollusks in the sauce. Cover and cook for 3 minutes.

Carefully lift the lid off the rondeau and, with a spider or slotted spoon, transfer any mollusks that have opened in the serving bowl. If some of the mollusks are still closed, replace the lid on the pot and cook for 1 or 2 more minutes. Transfer all the remaining opened mollusks to the serving bowl. Discard any that have not opened. Remove the bouquet garni and discard.

Decrease the heat to medium. Pierce the fennel with a knife, checking for doneness, and if they are tender, place them over the mollusks. Pour the hot sauce over the top and serve garnished with fennel fronds, accompanied by plenty of hot bread.

Salads

Baby Arugula Salad with Black Truffle Croque Monsieurs

Serves 4

Our *mise en place*, the set up of all necessary and preprepared ingredients for dinner service, includes a squeeze bottle of truffle oil and chilled leaves of baby arugula to garnish one of the fish dishes. Often at shift's end I slice open a warm, fresh sourdough roll, stuff it with arugula and a slice of whatever cheese is at hand, and lavishly sprinkle truffle oil over the whole thing. I sometimes crave these sandwiches on my day off, and I thought, "Hey, this could make a terrific salad." Here it is.

SWEET LEMON VINAIGRETTE

2 egg yolks

3 tablespoons freshly squeezed lemon juice

1 tablespoon champagne vinegar

1 teaspoon Dijon mustard

1 teaspoon minced shallot

1 tablespoon honey

1/3 cup extra virgin olive oil

Fleur de sel

Freshly cracked white pepper

ARUGULA SALAD

8 cups baby arugula leaves

1 Maui onion

CROQUE MONSIEURS

1/4 cup unsalted butter

8 thin slices sourdough bread, crusts trimmed

10 to 12 thin slices Fontinella cheese

32 thin slices black truffle, covered with a moist cloth

8 fresh Black Mission figs

To prepare the vinaigrette, combine the egg yolks, lemon juice, vinegar, mustard, shallot, and honey in a nonreactive bowl. Whip vigorously with a thin wire whisk until all the ingredients are thoroughly blended. Slowly drizzle the olive oil into the mixture, whipping continuously until all the olive oil is incorporated. The mixture will have a somewhat creamy consistency. Season with the sea salt and cracked white pepper.

To prepare the salad, gently wash and spin-dry the arugula, being very careful not to break the leaves. Transfer to a large bowl. Cover and refrigerate until ready to serve. Peel, and halve the onion. Slice very thinly with a sharp knife or mandoline.

To prepare the croque monsieurs, melt the butter in a small saucepan over low heat. Remove from the heat.

Using a 2-inch round cookie cutter, cut out 16 circles of the sourdough bread and 16 circles of Fontinella cheese. Brush both sides of the bread rounds with the melted butter and place in a baking pan. Place a cheese round on each circle of bread. Place 4 slices of truffle on 8 of the bread rounds and top with the remaining 8 bread circles, cheese side down, to create 8 sandwiches.

Prepare a plate with several layers of paper towels. Chill 4 dinner plates.

Place a nonstick pan over medium heat. When the pan is hot, transfer the croque monsieurs to the pan and toast each side for about 45 seconds, turning once, until lightly brown. Transfer to the paper towels to drain. Set in a warm place.

Halve the figs lengthwise and place 4 halves in a small cluster on each of the 4 plates. Remove the arugula from the refrigerator and add the onion. Whisk the vinaigrette back to consistency, and sprinkle three-quarters of the vinaigrette over the salad. Gently toss to coat. Form a tight mound of the salad on each plate. Place 2 of the warm croque monsieurs side by side, resting atop the salad. Encircle the salad mound with a light drizzling of the remaining dressing. Serve immediately.

Heirloom Tomatoes with Spanish Blue Cheese and Walnut "Pâté" with Fresh Herb Salad

Serves 4

One of the most exciting times of the summer months is the arrival of the heirloom vegetables. These marvelously diverse varieties, grown from ancient seedstock, of native, nonhybrid plants, have all their unique character intact: full flavor, deep color, unusual shape. Especially the tomatoes! We get inspired by the many different kinds: Zebra Greens, Purple Cherokees, Sweet 100s, and new ones we haven't tasted yet. This salad complements the ripe succulence of these tomatoes with the strong, exquisitely creamy blue cheese of Spain. We use Cabrales, but there are many delicious blues. The mock pâté is vegetarian and can be served on its own as an hors d'oeuvre with crisp water biscuits; the Cognac adds alluring fragrance. For this recipe, you will need a 12 by 24-inch sheet of parchment paper.

BLUE CHEESE AND WALNUT PÂTÉ

8 ounces Spanish blue cheese

2 tablespoons unsalted butter, at room temperature

$^1/_4$ cup heavy cream

2 tablespoons Cognac

2 tablespoons minced fresh chives

$^1/_2$ cup walnut pieces, toasted (page 219)

$^1/_2$ teaspoon sugar

2 teaspoons freshly ground white pepper

2 pounds mixed heirloom tomatoes, 6 to 8 small to medium tomatoes

$^1/_4$ cup extra virgin olive oil

$^1/_2$ teaspoon fleur de sel

Freshly ground black pepper

HERB SALAD

2 heads baby frisée, thoroughly washed and trimmed

12 small fresh basil leaves

12 fresh oregano leaves

Tender chive stems, 2 inches long

8 sprigs chervil

$^1/_2$ cup basic vinaigrette (page 203)

2 pinches fleur de sel

Pinch of freshly ground white pepper

Basil oil (page 204)

Balsamic reduction (page 203)

Place a small bowl and a wire whisk in the refrigerator to chill.

To prepare the pâté, combine the cheese and butter in a mixing bowl and mash with a wooden spoon. Remove the chilled bowl from the refrigerator and add the cream. Using the chilled whisk, whip the cream to soft peaks. Gently fold the whipped cream into the cheese mixture. Add the Cognac, chives, walnuts, sugar, and white pepper, and fold together to blend.

Shape the cheese pâté into an 8-inch log and place along the short side of a 12 by 24-inch piece of parchment paper, about 3 inches in from the edge, leaving 2 inches of paper on each end. Wrap the paper over the log, and roll the log inside the paper, forming a tube shape. Apply pressure evenly and wrap the pâté firmly in the parchment, making sure to keep the log smooth and round. Twist the paper ends tightly to seal. Refrigerate for at least 2 hours or overnight.

Remove from the refrigerator and unwrap the parchment from the chilled pâté. Using a thin-bladed knife, slice off 4 (1-inch) rounds. Transfer to a plate and cover.

Peel the tomatoes, following the instructions on page 219. Slice the peeled tomatoes thickly, about 4 slices per tomato, and arrange them in a baking pan. Drizzle the olive oil over the slices and turn to coat. Season with the salt and pepper.

To prepare the salad, place the frisée, basil, oregano, chives, and chervil in a large bowl. Slowly pour a fine stream of the well-whisked vinaigrette over the greens. Season with the salt and white pepper and toss gently.

Chill 4 salad plates.

Stack 3 to 5 slices of tomato on each salad plate, varying the color and size. Equally divide the herb salad into 4 portions, and place a small mound beside the tomatoes. Place small dots of the basil oil and balsamic reduction on the plate, and arrange the "pâté" rounds to create a visually pleasing triangle of salad, tomatoes, and pâté.

Mizuna Salad with Maple-Glazed Smithfield Ham and Creamy Buttermilk Hazelnut Vinaigrette

Serves 4

For this salad, we use mizuna lettuce. These deep green, saw-toothed leaves with a mild yet tangy flavor are sturdy enough to hold up when combined with the ham sautéed in butter browned to a nutlike richness and the sweet, velvety maple syrup that finishes the salad. The intense flavor of the Smithfield ham (see page 222) and the creamy, nutty vinaigrette make this salad rich and satisfying. Occasionally I add a grilled medallion of foie gras to this salad to create an even more decadent experience. Scatter the toasty hazelnuts atop right before serving, and voilà—a feast.

BUTTERMILK HAZELNUT VINAIGRETTE

3/4 cup fresh mayonnaise (page 209)

1/2 cup buttermilk

1 tablespoon cider vinegar

1 tablespoon finely chopped Italian parsley

1 teaspoon minced shallot

1/2 cup ground toasted (page 219) hazelnuts

1/2 teaspoon salt

1/2 teaspoon freshly ground white pepper

2 tablespoons unsalted butter

1 cup julienned Smithfield ham

1/2 cup split hazelnuts, toasted (page 219)

2 tablespoons thinly sliced Bermuda onion

2 tablespoons good-quality maple syrup

1/4 teaspoon freshly ground coarse black pepper

8 cups mizuna, washed and dried

To prepare the vinaigrette, in a nonreactive bowl, place the mayonnaise, buttermilk, and vinegar and whisk together until smooth. Add the parsley, shallot, hazelnuts, salt, and white pepper. Whisk until fully incorporated. Cover and set aside. If you have extra vinaigrette after dressing the salad, it will keep for up to 3 days, covered and refrigerated.

Chill 4 large salad plates.

To prepare the salad, place a sauté pan over medium heat and add the butter. When the butter has melted and turned golden brown, add the ham, hazelnuts, and onion. Sauté for about 2 minutes, until the onion starts to become translucent. Add the maple syrup and pepper and stir to coat. Cook for another 2 minutes, until the syrup has become sticky and slightly caramelized and clings to all the ingredients. Remove from the heat and set aside in a warm place.

Place the mizuna leaves in a large bowl. Whisk the vinaigrette again and pour half over the greens. Toss gently to coat all the leaves evenly. Add more of the vinaigrette as desired, to dress the greens to your liking.

Place a generous mound of the mizuna salad in the center of each plate. Spoon the sautéed ham on and around each salad. Serve immediately.

Baby Butter Lettuce with a Warm Heirloom Tomato and Goat Cheese Tart and Garlic Confit Vinaigrette

Serves 4

There is a little goat farm called Sweetwoods Dairy (see page 199) in Peña Blanca, New Mexico, where Patrice Inglis and her husband, Harrison Inglis, craft hand-made chèvre. We whip this superb goat cheese with a bit of aromatic olive oil and spring onions, then spread it on baked tart shells and lay thick slices of dewy, ruby-red heirloom tomatoes over the top. They're baked for only a few minutes, just to warm, but not cook, these delicate flavors. Then the whole dish is sprinkled with some fresh thyme leaves and a few drops of 25-year-old balsamico (see page 220). Ripe, organic heirloom or exceptional garden tomatoes are a must for this tart, which is perfect for a height-of-summer luncheon or brunch. You will need a small batch of puff pastry dough, which can be purchased, frozen, in any good grocery store, and four 4-inch tart pans *without* removable bottoms.

GARLIC CONFIT VINAIGRETTE

2 egg yolks

1 tablespoon garlic confit (page 208)

2 tablespoons sherry vinegar

1 teaspoon minced shallot

1/4 teaspoon brown sugar

1/4 cup extra virgin olive oil

1/2 teaspoon minced chives

1/2 teaspoon kosher salt

1/4 teaspoon freshly ground black pepper

1/2 teaspoon Dijon mustard

1/2 cup extra virgin olive oil

Kosher salt

4 (4-inch) circles of puff pastry dough, thawed but thoroughly chilled

1 cup good-quality fresh chèvre

2 tablespoons minced green onion

4 medium heirloom tomatoes, peeled (page 219) and cored

4 heads baby butter lettuce, split and washed (they are usually the size of an orange)

1 tablespoon aged balsamic vinegar, for garnish

1 tablespoon fresh thyme leaves, for garnish

To prepare the vinaigrette, combine the egg yolks, garlic confit, sherry vinegar, shallot, brown sugar, olive oil, chives, salt, pepper, and mustard in a blender and purée until smooth.

Preheat the oven to 400°F.

Arrange 4 (4-inch) tart pans (without removable bottoms) in a baking pan. Place a tablespoon of olive oil in each of the tart pans, and sprinkle a little salt into the oil. Carefully lay the circles of puff pastry in the pans, and lightly press them into the oil.

Place the pans in the center of the oven. Bake for 10 minutes, until the puff pastry has risen quite a bit and is golden brown. With a metal spatula, gently press down the puff pastry until it is even with the edges of the tart pans.

Return the tart shells to the oven, and bake for another 7 minutes, until golden brown. Remove from the oven, and let cool.

Leave the oven set at 400°F, for warming the tarts after they are filled.

In an electric mixer fitted with the paddle attachment, combine the chèvre, the remaining 1/4 cup olive oil, and the green onion and beat on medium speed until somewhat fluffy.

Using a very sharp knife, cut the tomatoes into ¹/₂-inch slices, being careful not to push out the seeds and pulp.

Line a baking pan with parchment paper.

Remove the puff pastry from the tart pans. Using a small spatula or a small butter knife, spread the goat cheese mixture in the bottoms of the tart shells. Arrange the tomato slices on top of the cheese. Place the tarts in the baking pan.

Chill 4 large salad plates.

Break off the leaves of the butter lettuce into a large bowl and discard the core and stem. Whisk the vinaigrette and sprinkle it over the lettuce. Toss gently, to thoroughly coat.

Place the tarts in the oven and bake for 3 minutes, just until warm.

Arrange the butter lettuce on the 4 plates in nice mounds that will provide a bed for the tart. Place a finished tart atop the lettuce on each plate. Place a few drops of the balsamic vinegar around the edge of the salad, and sprinkle the thyme leaves on the tarts. Serve immediately.

Italian Prosciutto Wrapped Baby Greens with Black Truffle Vinaigrette

Serves 4

My friend chef George Mahaffey taught me how to prepare dishes that are as visually dramatic as they are delicious. This signature salad is a variation of one I learned from him. The cured ham, earthy truffles, capers, cipollini onions, and tender greens make for a little vertical antipasto. It's entertaining to present this at the table because it looks a bit like a potted plant. Some diners wonder whether to lay it down or to try to cut it vertically. Some of the more adventurous just pick it up and take a bite. It's definitely an entertaining salad and makes a superb appetizer or light lunch with a family-style plate of Italian hard cheese and warm, crusty bread.

Unless you own a professional meat or deli slicer at home, you will need to have your butcher slice the prosciutto very thin, in long pieces. Make sure the slices are separated by wax paper.

BLACK TRUFFLE VINAIGRETTE

2 tablespoons apple cider vinegar

$1/2$ teaspoon honey

1 tablespoon very finely diced cipollini onion

1 tablespoon very finely diced black truffle

1 teaspoon very finely diced chives

1 teaspoon small nonpareil capers

$1/4$ cup light olive oil

1 tablespoon black or white truffle oil

$1/2$ teaspoon kosher salt

$1/4$ teaspoon freshly ground black pepper

1 head baby Lolla Rossa lettuce

1 head mizuna

1 head baby green-leaf lettuce

1 head baby romaine

8 thin slices of your favorite prosciutto, kept very cold

8 (4-inch) chive sticks

8 sprigs chervil

To prepare the vinaigrette, in a nonreactive bowl, combine the apple cider vinegar, honey, cipollini onion, black truffle, chives, and capers and whisk together. While whisking continuously, slowly drizzle in the olive oil and truffle oil. This emulsion breaks down quickly, so you will need to whisk it again before dressing the greens. This can be used immediately or made ahead, transferred to an airtight container, and refrigerated for up to 3 days.

To prepare the greens, separate the leaves of the baby lettuces. Place in a colander and wash well in cold water. Spin dry or gently pat dry with a clean towel.

On a clean working surface, lay out 2 slices of the chilled prosciutto horizontally, with one end overlapping the other by about 1 inch. The idea is to create a long strip of the prosciutto, so that when it is rolled up it has enough structural integrity to be freestanding.

Take one of each of the lettuce leaves, along with 2 sticks of chive and 2 sprigs of chervil, making sure all the tops are pointing in the same direction and the bottoms are gathered in a tidy little bunch. Lay the little bunch perpendicular to the strip of prosciutto, at one end. Whisk the vinaigrette and spoon a very small amount on the base of the

greens. Gently roll the prosciutto around the base of the greens so that the tops have a bouquet effect. Repeat this process 3 times.

Chill 4 salad plates.

With a sharp knife, trim the greens that extend past the bottom of the roll to form a flat surface, so that the roll stands up. Place a salad roll in the center of each of the 4 plates. Drizzle the vinaigrette over the salad and around the plate. Serve immediately.

Spring Dandelion Salad with Warm Crispy Shallots, Shaved Tuscan Pecorino, Quail Eggs, and Sweet Lemon and Tuscan Olive Oil Vinaigrette

Serves 4

I remember eating the first dandelion greens of spring at my grandfather's house. I can picture him vividly, out in his yard with a sharp little gardening spade, cutting what I thought were weeds, bringing them in the house, and tossing them into the sink. Before I knew it, they were in a bowl on the table, being doused with red wine vinegar, olive oil, and salt. My first bite of those "weeds" was a shock. They were so bitter, and the vinegar made them even more puckery. However, like many foods that I didn't enjoy on the first encounter, this one has became a great love of mine, especially as a celebration of the arrival of spring.

This salad is great served with hot Italian bread and a big spaghetti and meatball dinner. For this recipe, you will need a deep-fat fryer for the shallots, or a frying thermometer if you fry on your stovetop, and a mandoline or good-quality potato peeler to finely shave the cheese. The quail eggs need to be soaked in rice vinegar and refrigerated for 2 hours to facilitate peeling.

SWEET LEMON AND OLIVE OIL VINAIGRETTE

12 quail eggs

6 cups water

2 cups rice vinegar

1/3 cup freshly squeezed Meyer lemon juice

3/4 cup Tuscan extra virgin olive oil, or any other good-quality olive oil

2 tablespoons honey

Kosher salt

Freshly ground black pepper

4 peeled, thinly sliced fried shallots (page 208)

8 cups young dandelion leaves, washed and dried

Pinch of fleur de sel

8 ounces Tuscan pecorino

To prepare the quail eggs, place the eggs in a pot with the water, being careful not to crack the shells. Place the pot over medium-high heat and bring to a boil, reduce heat to medium low and boil for about 4 minutes. Remove from heat. Fill a bowl with 2 quarts of ice water. Using a slotted spoon, transfer the eggs to the ice water bath and shock for about 1 minute or until chilled. Transfer the eggs to a bowl, add the rice vinegar to cover, and refrigerate for 2 hours. Gently peel the eggs before using.

To prepare the vinaigrette, combine the lemon juice, olive oil, honey, and salt and pepper to taste in a nonreactive bowl and whisk together.

Have the fried shallots ready.

Place the dandelion greens in a large salad bowl and sprinkle with the lemon vinaigrette. Toss gently to coat thoroughly. Add the quail eggs, fried shallots, and fleur de sel. With a potato peeler or the mandoline, shave the pecorino cheese over the whole salad.

Summer Cherry Salad with Honey Vinaigrette

Serves 4

This very simple salad showcases the beauty of summer cherries. I don't think a summer season ever goes by when we don't have some kind of cherry in a salad at Geronimo. The luscious flavors, and the colors: yellow ones with brushes of amber, deep purple ones that reveal a rich syrup when you cut them, and fire engine red ones that are sweet and sour in perfect complement, and an aroma like no other. When they're at their peak, it is a treat for all the senses. I seldom, if ever, cook cherries, mostly because when they are ripe and wonderful, I can't see doing anything to interfere with their perfection. This salad is uncomplicated to make, but it requires juicy, marvelous cherries.

HONEY VINAIGRETTE

2 tablespoons rice vinegar

1 teaspoon minced shallot

1 tablespoon honey

1/4 cup light olive oil

1/2 teaspoon kosher salt

1/4 teaspoon freshly ground white pepper

40 ripe cherries

2 heads Belgian endive

2 bunches baby living watercress

Kosher salt

Combine the rice vinegar, shallot, honey, olive oil, salt, and white pepper in a nonreactive bowl and whisk together.

Stem, split, and pit the cherries.

Slice the Belgian endive in half lengthwise. Cut out the core, and separate the leaves. Once Belgian endive has been cut, the exposed edges will oxidize and rust. If you are going to prepare this salad a few hours ahead, soak the leaves in cold milk to preserve their color and crispiness. Make sure to dry them thoroughly before dressing.

Place the watercress in a colander. Wash in cold water and spin dry.

Chill 4 plates, if you are going to serve the salad in individual portions.

In a large bowl, combine the endive and watercress. Whisk the vinaigrette and sprinkle over the greens. Toss gently to coat thoroughly. Immediately before serving, toss in the cherries and serve as a large, family-style salad, or arrange on 4 chilled plates.

When I walk past a big Hobart ricer, churning, gears grinding as it pushes through warm potatoes, creating a smell uniquely its own—earthy, hot, and steamy—the buttery aroma always reminds me of the late Jimmy Burger.

Jimmy was the *entremettier*—in essence, the potato man. His sole job every day was to prepare the potatoes and vegetables for hundreds of people, for parties and banquets alike.

A funny little guy from the coal regions in Pennsylvania, literally, four foot something in height, he would stand in one spot, all day long, wearing wing-tip shoes on that hard, slick tile floor. I remember his shoes vividly because he was nearly always standing in a large puddle of water, and his shoes had soaked and dried so many times that the toes pointed straight up in the air. It was like working with an elf.

He was so good at what he did, though, that it was impossible to bring yourself to tease him.

Working with him gave me quite a repertoire of the classics. On any given day, we might have six different parties, each requiring a different potato and vegetable. We would make duchess potatoes, lorette potatoes, dauphinoise potatoes, cendrillon potatoes, fondant potatoes, and two or three different kinds of mashed potatoes. To this day, I have never again made that many kinds of potatoes all at once.

Jimmy could tournée a potato in a matter of seconds, holding it in one hand and, with a sharp paring knife, cut seven equal sides to create a football shape. He was also the commander of what we called the Potato Terminator. Actually, it was an electric potato peeler, a giant sandpaper cylinder that resembled a sideways Ferris wheel. Jim would pour bag after hundred-pound bag of enormous bull potatoes into this machine, and it would literally whittle them down to whatever size he desired.

I'll never forget my first turn at this monster. I got a little too sure of myself and left it unattended. I soon learned the power of the Terminator. When I opened the door of the machine, potatoes reduced to the size of marbles rolled out. Of course, at that moment, Rory Reno, the sous chef and the toughest guy in the kitchen, was standing right behind me. Needless to say, I never made that mistake again.

Eric on . . . Memory Lane: Jimmy B

Desserts

Pizzelle

Makes approximately 30 cookies

Coming home from school was always a treat when my mother was baking, and her anise pizzelle were by far my favorite. I'd sneak as many as I could, fill the pockets of my ski jacket, then quickly disappear to gorge on them in secret. It may seem that this version calls for a lot of anise; actually, however, they are perfect—wonderful hot off the iron and even better the next day, when the flavors have melded. And in the making, these delicate cookies will fill your house with enticing scents. You will need an electric pizzelle iron to make these cookies.

1 cup unsalted butter, at room temperature

1¹/₂ cups sugar

2 tablespoons anise oil

¹/₂ teaspoon salt

2 tablespoons minced lemon zest

2 tablespoons minced orange zest

2 tablespoons anise seeds toasted (page 219)

6 eggs

4¹/₂ cups all-purpose flour, sifted

2 teaspoons baking powder, sifted

Preheat an electric pizzelle iron.

In an electric mixer fitted with the paddle attachment, cream together the butter and sugar on low speed for about 2 minutes, until light and lemon-colored. Add the anise oil, salt, lemon zest, orange zest, and anise seed. Keeping the mixer on low, add the eggs one at a time and mix until smooth. Stop the machine and add all the sifted flour and baking powder at once. Mix again on low speed, scraping down the sides as necessary, just until the batter is formed. Do not overmix. Set the bowl of dough inside a larger bowl of ice water to keep it chilled while making the cookies.

Prepare a plate with several layers of paper towels. Open the lid of the pizzelle iron and drop about a teaspoon of the batter on the hot surface. Close the lid and cook for 1 to 2 minutes, or until golden brown. Getting the amount of batter and the timing just right may involve some trial and error. Transfer the baked pizzelle to the paper towels and cool. Repeat until all the batter has been baked.

Griddled "Elephant Heart" Plum Hotcakes with Rich Tahitian Vanilla Ice Cream

Serves 4

Elephant Heart plums are an old-time variety. Their skin is green and their flesh, which is exceptionally sweet and juicy, is bright red. Although they are becoming a rarity among commercial growers, because their delicate skin requires very gentle handling, they are worth seeking out. They are one of the best eating plums ever. I would never poach them or cook them for very long. Here we heat them briefly inside a hotcake to release their sugars and accentuate these simple pancakes, creating a comforting end to a fine meal. The cool, extra-rich vanilla ice cream continues the theme of homey yet subtly revved flavors. The Tahitian vanilla beans (see page 222) are especially moist and luscious and well worth searching out as well. You will need an ice cream machine to make this recipe.

TAHITIAN VANILLA ICE CREAM

5 egg yolks

$^2/_3$ cup sugar

1 cup half-and-half

2 tablespoons unsalted butter, at room temperature

1 cup heavy cream

1 Tahitian vanilla bean, split lengthwise, seeds scraped (page 212)

2 teaspoons vanilla extract

PLUM HOTCAKES

2 cups all-purpose flour

1 teaspoon cream of tartar

$^1/_2$ teaspoon baking soda

2 tablespoons superfine sugar

2 eggs

$1^1/_4$ cups buttermilk

$^1/_4$ cup unsalted butter, melted and browned

1 cup peeled, stoned, and medium-diced ripe Elephant Heart plums, about 4 plums

Canola oil, for oiling griddle

Powdered sugar, for garnish

Mint sprigs, for garnish

To prepare the ice cream, fill a saucepan about halfway full of water and place over medium heat. Bring the water to a boil.

Place the yolks and sugar in a small, heatproof bowl and whisk together until blended. Place the bowl over the boiling water. Add the half-and-half and stir. Cook and whisk over the boiling water for about 5 minutes, until nicely thickened.

Remove from the heat and set the bowl on a rack to cool. Stir in the butter. While the mixture cools, stir occasionally until it reaches room temperature. Stir in the heavy cream, the vanilla seeds, and the vanilla extract.

Freeze in an ice cream maker according to the manufacturer's directions. Cover tightly and store in the freezer.

To prepare the hotcakes, heat a griddle or large, nonstick skillet over medium heat.

Sift together the flour, cream of tartar, baking soda, and sugar into a bowl. Make a well in the flour mixture. In a separate small bowl, combine the eggs, buttermilk, and butter and stir just to mix. Pour the egg mixture into the center of the flour and whisk just until smooth. Do not overmix. Gently fold in the plums. Cover and refrigerate for 1 hour.

Set out a platter and a clean kitchen towel.

Heat a griddle over medium-high heat. Brush with canola oil. When the griddle is hot, ladle out enough batter, about 2 tablespoons, to make 3-inch hotcakes. Space them at least 2 inches apart. Cook for 1 or 2 minutes on each side, until golden brown. Transfer to the plate and cover with the towel as they come off the griddle. You should have about 12 pancakes.

Take the ice cream out of the freezer to let it soften a bit, and set out 4 shallow bowls.

Place a pancake in each bowl and top with tiny scoops of the ice cream. Add another pancake and another layer of ice cream. Top with a third pancake. Dust with the powdered sugar and garnish with the mint sprigs. Serve immediately.

Chocolate Tart

This is a marvelously simple but rich dessert. Sometimes at the end of a multicourse meal, I serve a thin slice of this tart without any sauces or garnishes, just fresh berries and an array of cheeses. For this recipe, you will need a 9-inch fluted tart pan with a removable bottom and some really good-quality dark chocolate. We use Valrhona, which is high on my list of excellent chocolates.

TART SHELL

1 egg yolk

1 vanilla bean, split lengthwise, seeds scraped (page 212)

$1/2$ cup powdered sugar

2 tablespoons whole blanched almonds

$3/4$ cup sifted all-purpose flour

Pinch of salt

5 tablespoons unsalted butter, at room temperature

DARK CHOCOLATE FILLING

$3/4$ cup heavy cream

$1/3$ cup milk

$1^1/4$ cups finely chopped high-quality dark chocolate

1 large egg, lightly beaten

1 teaspoon unsweetened Dutch cocoa powder

To prepare the tart shell, in a small bowl combine the egg yolk and the vanilla seeds. Whisk to blend. In a food processor, combine the sugar and almonds. Process until the nuts are finely ground. Add the flour and salt and process to blend. Add the butter and process until the mixture resembles coarse cornmeal. Add the egg yolk and vanilla seeds and pulse just until the dough begins to hold together. It's important not to overmix the dough; mix it just enough to pick up all the ingredients.

Using a rubber spatula, transfer the dough onto a large piece of plastic wrap and form it into a disk. Do not knead the dough. Wrap it tightly and refrigerate for at least 2 hours or overnight.

Butter a 9-inch fluted tart pan with a removable bottom.

Sprinkle a clean surface with flour. Using a lightly floured rolling pin, roll out the dough to form an 11-inch circle. The size need not be exact; it just needs to cover the tart pan. Gently fold the dough in half, and transfer it to the tart pan. Laying the crease in the center of the pan, unfold the dough. It should cover the pan, with about $1/2$ inch overlapping the rim. Gently fit the dough down into the tart pan and cut off the excess by lightly rolling your rolling pin over the top of the tart pan, cutting the edges. Using a fork, prick the tart bottom all over. Refrigerate for 1 hour.

Preheat the oven to 375°F.

Remove the tart shell from the refrigerator and place it in a baking pan. Place the pan in the center of the oven and bake for about 15 minutes, or until golden brown. Remove from the oven and set on a rack to cool.

To prepare the filling, place a heavy-bottomed saucepan over medium heat and add the cream and milk. Bring just to a simmer and remove from the heat. Add the chocolate and whisk until melted. Let cool for 5 minutes. Whisk in the egg and blend thoroughly.

Pour the filling into the pastry shell and place on the middle rack of the oven. Bake for 12 to 15 minutes, until the filling is somewhat set. Remove from the oven. Set on a rack and cool just to room temperature.

Dust with the cocoa powder. This dessert is best served at room temperature or even slightly warm.

Poire-Williams Soup with Warm Bosc Pears, Star Anise Ice Cream, and Black Pepper Génoise

Serves 6

When pears are in season, I love to buy a bushel of them and make this popular soup, which also works well on its own as a palate cleanser between courses. But the real treat is making the velvety soup, the exotic ice cream, the peppery, sweet cake, and the soft, warm pears and marrying them all together. This is a dessert that celebrates the spicy flavors of fall.

Génoise is a beautiful French pastry, leavened entirely by the air that is beaten into the eggs. Bringing the eggs to room temperature before preparing the cake will increase the volume of the eggs and ensure the lightness of the cake, as will taking great care when folding in the flour. The soup and ice cream can be made a day or two ahead of time.

Star Anise Ice Cream (page 166)

POIRE-WILLIAMS SOUP

2 cups water

1$^1/_2$ cups sugar

1 cup fresh apple cider

3 star anise pods

1$^1/_2$ whole allspice

3 cups peeled, cored, and diced ripe Bosc pears, about 4 medium pears

$^1/_4$ cup half-and-half

$^1/_4$ cup Poire-Williams brandy

BLACK PEPPER GÉNOISE

1 cup all-purpose flour

$^1/_2$ teaspoon baking powder

1$^1/_2$ teaspoons freshly ground black pepper

$^1/_2$ cup unsalted butter, at room temperature

$^1/_2$ cup sugar

2 eggs, at room temperature

$^1/_2$ teaspoon vanilla extract

SAUTÉED PEARS

2 tablespoons unsalted butter

2 ripe Bosc pears, peeled, cored, and diced

1 tablespoon brown sugar

$^1/_2$ teaspoon chopped fresh mint leaves

Pinch of kosher salt

Freshly grated cinnamon, for garnish

Prepare the ice cream, and freeze until ready to serve.

To prepare the soup, combine the water, sugar, apple cider, star anise, and allspice in a saucepan. Stir to dissolve the sugar. Place over medium-low heat and simmer for 15 minutes to concentrate the flavors. Remove from the heat. Strain through a sieve into a bowl and add the pears. Transfer back to the saucepan and simmer the pears in the syrup for about 7 minutes, until they are soft. Remove from the heat. Transfer to a blender and purée until smooth. Strain through a medium-hole china cap into a clean bowl and let cool to room temperature. Stir in the half-and-half and brandy. Cover and refrigerate until ready to serve.

Preheat the oven to 350°F. Butter an 8-inch square cake pan.

To prepare the génoise, sift together the flour, baking powder, and pepper in a small bowl. In an electric mixer fitted with the paddle attachment, cream together the butter and sugar on high speed for about 2 minutes, until light and lemon-colored. Beat in the eggs at high speed, until very light and fluffy. Remove the bowl from the mixer. Using a rubber spatula, gently fold the flour mixture into the batter. Stir in the vanilla. Pour the batter into the cake pan.

Place the pan in the center of the oven and bake for 20 to 30 minutes, until the cake is light golden brown and begins to pull away from the sides of the pan.

Remove from the oven and place on a wire rack. Cool for 10 minutes. Carefully remove the cake from the pan and lay a piece of plastic wrap over the cake.

Remove the ice cream from the freezer and allow to soften slightly.

To prepare the sautéed pears, place a sauté pan over medium heat and add the butter. When the butter is bubbly, add the pears, brown sugar, mint, and salt. Sauté for 1 minute and remove from the heat.

To finish, cut the génoise into 6 squares and place a square in each of 6 soup bowls.

Place a scoop of the ice cream atop each square of cake. Spoon some of the sautéed pears over the ice cream and ladle about $1/2$ cup of the soup around the cake. Sprinkle with grated cinnamon and serve immediately.

Star Anise Ice Cream

Makes about 1 quart

This ice cream is for those closet licorice lovers, of which I am one.

5 large egg yolks
3/4 cup sugar
2 cups whole milk
5 star anise pods, crushed coarsely in a mortar with a pestle
1 cup half-and-half
1 teaspoon vanilla extract

In the bowl of an electric mixer, combine the egg yolks and sugar. Using the whisk attachment beat at medium-high speed, until the mixture is thick and pale yellow in color. Remove the bowl from the mixer.

Place a saucepan over medium heat. Add the milk and star anise and bring to a simmer. Remove from the heat.

Add half of the milk to the egg yolk mixture and whisk until blended. Add the remaining milk and stir. Transfer the mixture back to the saucepan, and place over medium-low heat. Cook, stirring constantly, for about 5 minutes, until the mixture coats the back of a spoon. Remove from the heat.

Stir in the half-and-half. Pass the mixture through a fine strainer into a bowl. Set the bowl over a larger bowl filled with ice water and chill. Stir in the vanilla extract. Freeze in an ice cream maker according to the manufacturer's instructions.

Serve the ice cream immediately, or store it in an airtight container in the freezer.

Meyer Lemon Semifreddo with Basil Seed Sauce

Serves 4

You may have noticed that many of the recipes in this book call for Meyer lemons. I have a special affinity for them, as do many of the gourmands who regularly come to Geronimo. This fruit is lemon, but sweeter. It was brought to the United States from China in 1908 by Frank N. Meyer, who had been hired by the U.S. Department of Agriculture to find new varieties of fruit unknown to the Western world. As he was preparing to return to the United States, Meyer found a curious citrus tree growing as a potted plant in a dooryard in Beijing. He obtained the specimen and brought it home with him, and thus we now have the "Meyer lemon."

This recipe is a little complex but is very doable. It calls for an unusual ingredient: basil seeds. The texture of basil seeds is quite interesting, similar to very tender tapioca. To make the semifreddo, which resembles a partially frozen mousse, you will need a candy thermometer, a pastry bag with a large round tip, and 4 metal ring molds, 1 inch in diameter and 4 inches tall. The semifreddo needs to be refrigerated for 8 hours before serving.

LEMON CURD

Grated zest of 2 lemons

$1/2$ cup freshly squeezed Meyer lemon juice

$1/2$ cup sugar

2 eggs

1 egg yolk

$1/2$ cup unsalted butter, cut into 1-inch cubes and refrigerated

ITALIAN MERINGUE

$1/4$ cup water

$3/4$ cup sugar

4 egg whites

BASIL SEED SAUCE

$1^1/2$ cups basil seeds

$1/4$ cup simple syrup (page 211)

$1/2$ cup dry white wine

Tiny basil leaves, for garnish

Meyer lemon segments, for garnish

To prepare the lemon curd, bring a large pot of water to a boil over medium heat. Combine the lemon zest, lemon juice, sugar, eggs, and yolk in a metal bowl and set over the boiling water. Cook, whisking constantly, for about 5 minutes, until very thick. With a rubber spatula, thoroughly scrape down the sides of the bowl as the mixture cooks, to prevent the eggs from scrambling. Remove from the heat and whisk in the butter until it is completely melted. Strain through a chinois into a large bowl. Set over a larger bowl filled with ice water, and chill.

To prepare the Italian meringue, place a heavy-bottomed pot over medium-high heat and add the water and sugar. Stir to mix thoroughly. Brush the sides of the pan down with a clean pastry brush dipped in water to dissolve any sugar crystals, and continue brushing down the sides if crystals form while cooking. Cook for 10 to 15 minutes, until it reaches the soft-ball stage, 234°F to 240°F.

Make sure the bowl and whip attachment of the electric mixer are thoroughly clean, the egg whites won't whip properly if any grease is present in the bowl.

In an electric mixer fitted with the whip attachment, whip the egg whites on high speed until they are doubled in volume.

When the sugar has reached the proper temperature, very, very slowly add it to the doubled whites in a thin stream, continuing to whip the egg whites on high speed. If you add the syrup too quickly, the eggs will cook too fast and lose all of their volume. Whip the meringue until the bowl is cool to the touch. It should almost quadruple in volume.

In 3 additions, gently fold the Italian meringue into the lemon curd.

Line a baking pan with parchment paper, and place 4 metal ring molds, 1 inch in diameter and 4 inches tall, upright in the pan. Fill a pastry bag with the lemon mousse. Carefully pipe the mousse into the ring molds, filling them to the top. Cover and freeze for at least 8 hours.

To prepare the sauce, rinse the basil seeds in a chinois under cold running water. Place in a bowl and stir in the simple syrup and white wine. Cover and refrigerate until thoroughly chilled.

Chill 4 deep plates.

To serve, spoon some of the sauce into the bottom of each plate.

Remove the semifreddos from the freezer. Heat the molds gently with a little butane torch, or wrap them in a warm, damp cloth. Gently slide the molds off and stand a semifreddo in the center of each plate.

Garnish with the basil leaves and lemon segments. Serve immediately.

El Ray Venezuelan Milk Chocolate Mousse Pies with Macadamia Nut Crust and Caramelized Bananas

Serves 4

We wanted something to highlight the smoothness of one of my favorite eating chocolates, the Venezuelan milk chocolate from El Ray. Kevin Reinhold, our pastry chef, came up with this dessert, and it has become a regular player on the menu. This recipe does contain quite a few steps, and it is easier if done in stages or even a day ahead. For instance, the day before you plan to serve this, make the macadamia filling and the pâte sucrée. You will need four 6-inch tart pans with removable bottoms, a candy thermometer, and a small hand-held torch to caramelize the bananas.

MACADAMIA FILLING

$^1/_4$ cup sugar

1 tablespoon plus 1 teaspoon water

$1^1/_2$ teaspoons freshly squeezed lemon juice

$^1/_4$ cup heavy cream, at room temperature

$^1/_2$ cup finely chopped raw macadamia nuts

CHOCOLATE PÂTE SUCRÉE

$^1/_4$ cup unsalted butter, at room temperature

1 vanilla bean, split lengthwise, seeds scraped (page 212)

$^3/_4$ cup sugar

$^1/_8$ teaspoon salt

1 egg yolk

1 cup pastry flour

$^1/_3$ cup unsweetened cocoa powder

2 tablespoons unsweetened Dutch cocoa powder mixed with 2 tablespoons flour, for rolling out the dough

MILK CHOCOLATE MOUSSE

$^1/_3$ cup finely chopped milk chocolate

1 egg

2 egg yolks

1 tablespoon water

$^1/_4$ cup sugar

$^1/_3$ cup plus 2 tablespoons heavy cream

2 ripe bananas

$^1/_4$ cup superfine sugar

To prepare the macadamia filling, place a saucepan over medium heat and add the sugar, water, and lemon juice. Stir to dissolve the sugar. Cook for about 5 minutes, until it turns a dark mahogany color. Slowly add the cream to the cooked sugar, whisking constantly. Use caution, as the warm cream will bubble up and release steam. Remove from the heat. Let the filling cool completely. Add the nuts and cover.

To prepare the pâte sucrée, combine the butter, vanilla seeds, sugar, salt, egg yolk, flour, and cocoa powder in the bowl of an electric mixer. Using the dough hook attachment, mix at low speed for about 1 minute, until the dough pulls away from the sides. Do not overmix. Using a rubber spatula, transfer the dough onto a sheet of plastic wrap and wrap tightly. Refrigerate for 1 hour.

Set out (6-inch) tart pans with removable bottoms.

Sprinkle a clean surface with the flour and cocoa powder mixture. Remove the dough from the refrigerator, and cut it into 4 equal pieces. It is important to work with the dough while cold.

Using a rolling pin dusted with the flour and cocoa mixture, roll each piece into a circle 6 inches across and $^1/_4$ inch thick. With a fork, prick 4 or 5 rows of holes randomly over the surface of each dough circle. Carefully fit the dough rounds into the bottoms of the tart pans and press them snugly into the sides. Cut the overhanging dough off, level with the pan's edge.

Cover and refrigerate for 15 minutes.

Set out a baking pan, and preheat the oven to 325°F.

Remove the tart shells from the refrigerator, and transfer them to the baking pan. Place in the oven and bake for about 8 minutes, until slightly firm.

Remove the tart shells from the oven, leaving them in the baking pan. Spoon 1 tablespoon of the macadamia filling into each shell, and return the shells to the oven. Bake for an additional 5 minutes, until the nut mixture has melted to cover the bottom of the tart. Remove from the oven. Set on a rack to cool.

To prepare the mousse, fill a small saucepan halfway with water and place over medium heat. Bring the water to a simmer and set a small heat-proof bowl over the pot. Place the chopped chocolate in the bowl and stir frequently until the chocolate is completely melted. Remove from the heat and set in a warm place.

In an electric mixer fitted with the whip attachment, whip the egg and yolks on high speed for about 3 minutes, until doubled in volume and pale in color. Place a very small saucepan over medium heat and add the water and sugar. Brush the sides of the pan down with a clean pastry brush dipped in

water to dissolve any sugar crystals, and continue brushing down the sides if crystals form while cooking. Cook for 10 to 15 minutes, until a thick syrup forms and the mixture has reached the soft-ball stage, 234°F to 240°F. With the mixer running on medium speed, slowly add the syrup to the whipped eggs in a thin stream. Continue to whip on medium speed for about 5 minutes, until the bowl is cool to the touch.

Using a rubber spatula, fold the melted chocolate slowly into the eggs, until integrated. Transfer to a large bowl and cover.

In an electric mixer fitted with the whip attachment, whip the heavy cream on medium-high speed for about 2 minutes, until it forms soft peaks.

Very gently fold the cream into the chocolate and egg mixture. Do not beat. This will allow the ingredients to hold their volume and create a light mousse. Cover and refrigerate for about 2 hours, until set.

When the tart shells are cool, pop them out of the pans and set them on a tray.

Scoop 1/4 cup of the mousse into each shell, and spread the mousse flush with the top of the shell. Refrigerate the filled tarts for 1 hour.

Peel the bananas and slice them 1/4 inch thick. Overlap the slices in concentric circles to cover the surface of the tart. Sprinkle the superfine sugar evenly on top of the bananas and caramelize with a brûlée torch. Serve immediately.

Pistachio Ice Cream

Makes 3 cups

Judyth has always loved pistachio ice cream. When she was a kid, it felt very gourmet, like being the only one of her friends who liked oysters, sweetbreads, and black licorice. Pistachio ice cream was also the perfect and necessary ending to the Sunday night Chinese restaurant dinners of her New York City childhood, where her fondness for it began. This recipe makes a really grand version, rich and nutty, and amazingly, the ice cream is not green!

3/4 cup unsalted shelled pistachios

3/4 cup sugar

1 cup milk

1 cup half-and-half

1 teaspoon almond extract

Pinch of salt

5 large egg yolks

Combine the pistachios and 1/4 cup of the sugar in a food processor, and grind to a very fine powder. Place a heavy-bottomed saucepan over medium heat. Add the pistachio mixture, milk, half-and-half, almond extract, and salt. Stir and bring to a boil. Remove from the heat.

In a large bowl, whisk together the yolks and the remaining 1/2 cup sugar until well blended.

Slowly, in small additions, whisk the hot pistachio milk mixture into the yolk mixture.

Transfer the mixture to the saucepan and place over medium-low heat. Cook for about 8 minutes, stirring constantly, until the custard thickens slightly and clings to the back of a spoon. Be careful not to boil. Remove from the heat.

Pour the custard into a large bowl, and set it over a larger bowl filled with ice water for about 15 minutes, stirring frequently, until cold.

Freeze the custard in an ice cream maker, according to the manufacturer's instructions.

Serve immediately, or store in an airtight container in the freezer for up to 1 week.

Toasted Coconut Shortbread with Cinnamon Ice Cream and Caramel Apple Sabayon

Serves 4

Caramel apples! When I was a kid I used to get them at a local amusement park. Once I got a whiff of the hot caramel, there was no resisting. Caramel was stuck between my teeth for the rest of the night, but it was so worth it. The sabayon in this dessert has some of that flavor, and it really weds the shortbread and cinnamon ice cream.

CINNAMON ICE CREAM

3 cups heavy cream

1¹/₂ cups whole milk

2 vanilla beans, split lengthwise, seeds scraped (page 212)

1 cup plus 2 tablespoons sugar

6 egg yolks

2¹/₂ teaspoons freshly ground cinnamon

TOASTED COCONUT SHORTBREAD

¹/₂ cup cold unsalted butter

3 tablespoons sugar

1 egg yolk

¹/₄ teaspoon vanilla extract

¹/₂ vanilla bean, split lengthwise, seeds scraped (page 212)

1 cup high-gluten flour

2 tablespoons shredded coconut, toasted (page 219)

CARAMEL APPLE SABAYON

2 tablespoons unsalted butter

3 tablespoons sugar

³/₄ cup very finely diced peeled Granny Smith apple

Pinch of kosher salt

6 egg yolks

¹/₂ cup superfine sugar

²/₃ cup Calvados (apple brandy)

1 tablespoon apple syrup (page 203)

¹/₂ Granny Smith apple, julienned, for garnish

To prepare the cinnamon ice cream, combine the cream and milk in a large saucepan and place over medium heat. Add the vanilla seeds and pod. Bring just to a simmer. Remove from the heat.

Combine the sugar and egg yolks in large bowl and whisk to blend. Gradually whisk in the hot cream mixture, adding a little at a time. Transfer back into the same saucepan. Place over medium-low heat and cook for about 6 minutes, stirring constantly, until the custard thickens and coats the back of a spoon. Take care not to boil the custard. Strain through a chinois into a large bowl. Whisk in the cinnamon.

Freeze the custard in an ice cream maker, according to the manufacturer's instructions. Cover tightly and store in the freezer until ready to serve.

To prepare the shortbread, in an electric mixer fitted with the paddle attachment, cream together the butter and sugar on low speed just until incorporated. Add the egg yolk, vanilla extract, and vanilla seeds and mix just to combine.

Turn off the mixer and add ¹/₄ cup of the flour. Start the mixer again on slow speed and add the remaining flour at ¹/4-cup intervals, mixing just until incorporated. Do not overmix.

Add the toasted coconut and mix just until it is evenly distributed throughout the dough.

The dough should be a little crumbly. Transfer it to a sheet of plastic wrap and wrap tightly. Refrigerate for 1 hour.

Preheat the oven to 300°F. Line a baking pan with parchment paper.

Sprinkle a clean surface with flour. Using a rolling pin lightly dusted with flour, gently roll out the dough about $1/4$ inch thick. Using a 2-inch round cookie cutter, cut the dough into 8 circles and place in the baking pan. Refrigerate for 15 minutes.

Place the pan in the oven and bake the shortbread for 8 to 12 minutes, until slightly firmed and without color.

To prepare the sabayon, place a sauté pan over medium heat and add the butter and sugar. Cook, stirring constantly with a wooden spoon, for about 1 minute, until the sugar begins to caramelize. Add the apple and salt. Continue to cook and stir for 2 minutes, until the apple is caramelized and coated with the sticky syrup. Remove from the heat. Set aside to cool to room temperature.

Place a pot of water over medium-high heat. When the water is very hot, but not boiling, place the egg yolks and superfine sugar in a heatproof bowl and set over the pot of water.

Cook and whisk for 5 minutes, until foamy and thick. Whisking continuously, slowly add the Calvados and apple syrup. Continue whisking for about 5 minutes, until light and pale in color.

Remove from the heat and set in a warm place.

Set out 4 dessert plates. Take the ice cream out of the freezer to soften a bit.

To assemble the dessert, set one of the shortbread cookies on each of the plates. Scoop a dollop of the cinnamon ice cream, about $1/4$ cup, on top of the cookie, place another cookie on top of the ice cream, and then add another dollop of the ice cream atop that. Fold together the caramelized apples and the sabayon and spoon generously over the ice cream and cookie. Garnish with the julienned apple, and serve immediately.

Eggnog Crème Brûlée with Burgundy Poached Seckel Pears

Serves 6

It never fails. The classics still call forth "mmmmmm" when it comes to the dessert course: chocolate cake, pumpkin pie, and, of course, the classic crème brûlée, literally burnt cream. We add a little twist and flavor it to suggest one of my favorite winter drinks, eggnog. The nutmeg and brandy give the custard the flavor of winter romance. We serve it with Seckel pears, which are small, beautifully shaped, firm-fleshed pears that hold up well in the spicy Burgundy syrup. This dessert offers a visually exciting yet pleasurably homey end to a dinner. You will need some ceramic ramekins for the brûlée custard. The pears will need to poach, and the custard needs to chill for at least 2 hours. They both may be prepared up to a day ahead.

POACHED BURGUNDY PEARS

6 cups red Burgundy wine

1 cup port wine

1 cup orange juice

1$^1/_2$ cups sugar

6 star anise pods

1 vanilla bean, split lengthwise, seeds scraped (page 212)

2 cinnamon sticks

12 tournée (page 219) or simply peeled ripe Seckel pears, stems intact

EGGNOG CRÈME BRÛLÉE

8 egg yolks

$^1/_4$ cup granulated sugar

$^1/_4$ cup firmly packed brown sugar

2 cups heavy cream

$^1/_2$ teaspoon freshly grated nutmeg

1 teaspoon brandy

1 teaspoon vanilla extract

$^1/_4$ cup granulated sugar, for caramelizing the tops

To poach the pears, combine the Burgundy, port, orange juice, sugar, star anise, vanilla seeds and pod, and cinnamon sticks in a large saucepan. Place over medium-high heat and bring to a simmer. Decrease the heat to medium-low to maintain a slow simmer. Add the pears and simmer for 20 minutes, until the tip of a paring knife slides easily through the bottom of the pear to the core. Using a slotted spoon, carefully remove the pears and set aside to cool in a bowl, with the stems pointing upward.

Continue to cook the Burgundy mixture for about 20 minutes, until the liquid is reduced by half. Remove from the heat and strain through a chinois into a bowl. Pour the liquid over the pears. Cover and refrigerate for at least 2 hours.

Preheat the oven to 300°F.

To prepare the crème brûlée, in a large bowl, whisk together the egg yolks, granulated sugar, and brown sugar until the sugar has dissolved and the mixture is thick and pale yellow. Add the cream, nutmeg, brandy, and vanilla and whisk until well blended. Strain through a chinois into a clean, large bowl.

Divide the mixture among 6 ramekins, 2 inches deep by 3 inches high. Place in a large roasting pan and fill the pan with water about halfway up the sides of the ramekins. Place in the oven and bake for 50 to 60 minutes, until set around the edges but still a bit loose in the center. Remove from the oven, and leave the ramekins in the roasting pan until cooled to room temperature. Then remove the ramekins from the pan, cover, and refrigerate for at least 2 hours.

Remove the pears from the refrigerator and arrange them in a shallow bowl with the stems pointing up. Place the syrupy poaching liquid in a sauceboat, to ladle over the pears and the brûlée. Cover and set aside.

When ready to serve, sprinkle about 2 teaspoons of sugar over each custard. For best results, use a small, hand-held torch to caramelize the sugar. If you don't have a torch, place the ramekins under a very hot broiler for a short time, until the sugar caramelizes.

For a dramatic presentation, we set each brûlée on a doily, on a plate for each guest, and serve the pears whole, family-style, in the middle of the table.

Chocolate and Cinnamon Pound Cake Pudding

Serves 6

This decadent pudding is pure comfort food. Make sure you use a high-quality chocolate; we use Valrhona. You will need to allow 24 hours to make this recipe; the cake will need to dry out for 12 hours.

CHOCOLATE BUTTERMILK CAKE

3/4 cup plus 1 tablespoon all-purpose flour

1/4 cup unsweetened Dutch cocoa powder

1/2 cup sugar

1/2 teaspoon salt

1/2 cup buttermilk

1/2 teaspoon vegetable oil

1 teaspoon vanilla extract

1/2 cup finely chopped high-quality milk chocolate

CINNAMON POUND CAKE

1 cup unsalted butter, at room temperature

1 1/2 cups plus 2 tablespoons sugar

5 eggs

1 tablespoon vanilla extract

2 cups cake flour, sifted

1 teaspoon freshly ground cinnamon

1/2 teaspoon salt

Cinnamon syrup (page 205)

CUSTARD

1/2 cup milk

2 1/2 cups heavy cream

1/4 cup firmly packed brown sugar

1/2 cup granulated sugar

1 vanilla bean, split lengthwise, seeds scraped (page 212)

6 egg yolks

Pistachio ice cream (page 172)

1/2 cup high-quality bittersweet chocolate shavings, for garnish

Preheat the oven to 325°F. Butter and flour a 10-inch round cake pan.

To prepare the buttermilk cake, in a large bowl, sift together the flour, cocoa powder, sugar, and salt. Make a well in the flour. Pour the buttermilk, vegetable oil, and vanilla into the center of the well. Mix all the ingredients together until smooth.

Pour the batter into the prepared cake pan and level the top. Sprinkle the chocolate over the cake batter. Place in the oven and bake for 25 to 30 minutes, or until a skewer inserted in the center comes out clean. Remove from the oven and set on a rack to cool. This makes a small layer of cake to be used in the pudding.

Keep the oven at 325°F. Butter and flour a second 10-inch round cake pan.

To prepare the cinnamon pound cake, in an electric mixer fitted with the paddle attachment, cream together the butter and sugar on medium speed for about 2 minutes, until light and fluffy. When doubled in volume, decrease the mixer speed to low and add the eggs, one at a time.

When the eggs are incorporated, add the vanilla and mix just until blended. Sift together the flour, cinnamon, and salt. Turn off the machine, and add one-third of the flour mixture. Turn the mixer to low speed and mix to blend. Blend in the remaining flour in 2 additions.

Pour the batter into the prepared cake pan, tap the pan on the counter to level the batter, and bake for 20 to 30 minutes, or until a skewer inserted in the center comes out clean. Brush with the cinnamon syrup, and place on a rack to cool.

To prepare the custard, combine the milk, cream, brown and granulated sugars, and vanilla seeds in a saucepan and place over medium heat. Cook for about 5 minutes, stirring constantly, until just boiling. Remove from the heat. Whisk in the egg yolks and strain through a fine sieve into a clean bowl. Cover and let cool completely, then refrigerate until ready to use.

Remove both cakes from their pans and set on a rack to dry out for 12 hours. Do not cover. After they have dried, cut the cakes into 1/2-inch squares.

Spray a 10-inch round cake pan with nonstick vegetable spray.

Lay the diced cake pieces in the pan, just to fill it. You may have a bit of extra cake left over, depending on the depth of your cake pan.

Preheat the oven to 300°F.

Pour the custard over the diced cake pieces and let rest for 10 minutes so they can absorb the liquid. Place a sheet of plastic wrap tightly across the top of the pan, and top that with a slightly larger piece of aluminum foil. There should be no plastic showing. Place the cake pan into a larger, ovenproof container, such as a roasting pan, with high sides. Fill the larger container with warm water one-third of the way up the sides of the cake pan.

Place in the oven and bake for 50 minutes to 1 hour, or until the middle has set. Remove from the oven and the water bath. Cool for 15 minutes before serving.

Serve a square of the warm cake with a scoop of pistachio ice cream, and garnish with chocolate shavings.

Flourless Chocolate Cakes with White Chocolate Vanilla Sauce

Serves 6

This is one of those "Let's share a dessert" desserts. It's beyond rich and will satisfy almost any chocoholic. The cake is very easy to make and will keep for a few days, tightly covered, in the refrigerator. You will need six 3-inch steel ring molds.

FLOURLESS CHOCOLATE CAKES

3 cups finely chopped high-quality semisweet chocolate

1 cup unsalted butter, cut into 1-inch pieces

6 eggs

2 egg yolks

$1/2$ cup sugar

WHITE CHOCOLATE VANILLA SAUCE

$1/4$ cup sugar

$1/4$ cup water

1 Tahitian vanilla bean, split lengthwise, seeds scraped (page 212)

2 cups very finely chopped high-quality white couverture chocolate

6 tablespoons heavy cream

Edible gold leaf, for garnish

Preheat the oven to 300°F. Line a baking pan with parchment paper. Oil the inside of 6 (3-inch) steel ring molds, and set them in the baking pan.

To prepare the cakes, place a pot of water over medium-low heat. When the water is very hot, but not boiling, place the chocolate and butter in a heatproof bowl and set over the pot of water until melted. Stir the chocolate and butter together, and remove from the heat. Set aside to cool at room temperature.

In an electric mixer fitted with the whip attachment, whip the eggs, egg yolks, and sugar on high speed for about 5 minutes, until doubled in volume.

Using a rubber spatula, fold the chocolate mixture into the egg mixture until smooth. Be careful not to deflate the volume.

Divide the mixture evenly among the ring molds and place in the oven. Bake for 30 to 35 minutes, until the eggs have set but the cakes are still soft. Place the pan on a rack to cool for 1 hour. Before unmolding, refrigerate the cakes for at least 2 hours. It's best to work with the cakes when they are cold.

To prepare the sauce, combine the sugar, water, and vanilla seeds in a heavy-bottomed saucepan. Place over medium heat and bring to a boil. Boil for 1 minute, until the flavors meld. Remove from the heat and add the chocolate. Stir until smooth. Add the heavy cream and stir until smooth.

Set out 6 dessert plates.

To unmold the cakes, gently run a thin-bladed knife around the inside of the ring mold, and lift the mold up and off the cake. Carefully place a cake on each plate. Spoon a small puddle of the sauce next to the cake, and garnish with the gold leaf.

Velarde Apple Normandy

Serves 12

The small northern New Mexico village of Velarde is justifiably renowned for its old, well-tended, heirloom orchards. Every fall, our roadside stands are lined with a kaleidoscope of offerings: brilliant crimson *ristras* of red chiles, huge *calabacitas,* braids of *ajo,* baskets of *cebollas,* and bushels and bushels of fresh apples. To honor this most local of small pleasures, we've come up with this cheesecake of sorts, with the snap of crisp apples and a bit of the old-timey zing of applejack brandy. You will need a 10-inch springform pan to make this cake, and the cake needs to chill overnight before being cut.

CRUST

3 cups graham cracker crumbs

$1/2$ cup unsalted butter, melted

FILLING

4 (8 ounces each) packages cream cheese

2 cups sugar

2 teaspoons vanilla extract

8 eggs

2 tablespoons ground cinnamon

$1/2$ cup all-purpose flour, sifted

6 tablespoons applejack brandy

2 Golden Delicious apples

To prepare the crust, in a bowl, mix together the graham cracker crumbs and butter. Pack the crumbs onto the bottom and three-fourths of the way up the sides of a 10-inch springform pan, and set aside.

Preheat the oven to 300°F.

To prepare the filling, in an electric mixer fitted with the paddle attachment, beat together the cream cheese, sugar, and vanilla on medium speed for about 2 minutes, until well blended.

Add the eggs, one at a time, until smooth and slightly liquefied. In a separate small bowl, stir the cinnamon into the flour with a fork. Set the mixer speed to low and add the flour to the batter. Add the brandy and mix just to blend.

Pour the batter into the prepared springform pan.

Peel and core the apples and slice into half moons. Fan them out on top of the batter.

Place in the oven and bake for 1 hour, until the center is set and the surface is golden brown. Remove from the oven and place on a rack to cool for at least 1 hour. Cover and refrigerate overnight. Remove from the refrigerator 1 hour before serving.

Run a thin-bladed knife between the cake and the inside of the springform. Release the sides of the springform pan, unmolding the cake. Dip a serrated cake knife into warm water, and wipe dry. Slice the cake into 12 slices.

White Peach Shortcake with Warm Buttermilk Biscuits and Honey Crema

Serves 6

Ripe white peaches are another one of those perfect fruits of summer. I love to treat them with great simplicity, because they are incredibly luscious as is, fresh and untouched. Here we have attempted to create a dessert that complements the purity of the peaches by pairing their delectable ultra-sweetness with a rich, slightly tangy *crema*, which is actually a version of crème fraîche. You will need to allow 12 hours to make the crema.

HONEY CREMA

1 cup heavy cream (40 percent butterfat)

2 tablespoons cultured buttermilk

2 tablespoons honey

Dash of vanilla extract

4 medium perfectly ripe white or yellow peaches

$1/2$ cup superfine sugar

1 tablespoon kirschwasser (cherry brandy)

BUTTERMILK BISCUITS

2 cups all-purpose flour

1 tablespoon baking powder

$3/4$ teaspoon salt

1 teaspoon sugar

$1/2$ teaspoon baking soda

5 tablespoons cold, unsalted butter

1 cup buttermilk

1 egg

2 tablespoons turbinado sugar

To prepare the crema, in a small nonreactive bowl, gently stir together the heavy cream and buttermilk. Cover the bowl loosely and allow it to stand at room temperature, 70°F, for 12 hours. Whisk in the honey and vanilla. Cover and refrigerate. The crema will keep for 1 week.

To prepare the peaches, peel, halve, and pit the fruit. Slice the peach halves into $1/2$-inch moons,

and place in a bowl. Pour the sugar and kirschwasser on the peaches and, with a gentle folding motion, coat the peaches, being careful not to bruise them. Cover and refrigerate for at least 1 hour. They can be held for up to 8 hours.

Preheat the oven to 425°F.

To prepare the biscuits, in a large bowl, sift together the flour, baking powder, salt, sugar, and baking soda. Using a pastry blender or a large-tined fork, blend the butter into the flour mixture until coarse crumbs form. Add the buttermilk. Fold lightly with a fork until the dough forms a ball.

With a rubber spatula, transfer the dough onto a lightly floured surface. With your hands, gently knead a few times just until combined, not perfectly smooth like a bread or pasta dough. Biscuit dough can easily be over mixed and toughened, because there are no eggs to tenderize it. The less you handle it, the flakier and lighter the biscuits will be.

Line a baking sheet with parchment paper. In a small bowl, whip the egg with a fork.

Sprinkle a clean surface with flour. Using a lightly floured rolling pin, gently roll out the dough to a $3/4$-inch thickness. Using a 3-inch biscuit cutter dipped in flour, cut out biscuits as close together as possible. Place the biscuits 2 inches apart on the baking sheet. Brush with the egg wash and sprinkle with the sugar. Place in the oven and bake for 12 to 15 minutes, until golden. Remove from the oven.

Remove the crema and the peaches from the refrigerator.

While the biscuits are still warm, carefully slice them in half and place the bottom halves in shallow dessert bowls. Spoon a small dollop of the crema on each bottom half. Using a slotted spoon, arrange a generous spoonful of peaches atop the crema. Spoon a little more crema on the peaches, and top with the other half of the biscuit.

Drizzle with a little of the syrup from the peaches. Serve immediately.

Throughout the writing of this book, it has been a pleasure to recollect the many experiences and the many people who have helped me understand in my mind, palate, and heart what the love of food and hospitality is really about. In this regard and many others, Cliff Skoglund has been a powerful mentor to me.

My Santa Fe life began with a job that Daniel Boulud had arranged for me: running the kitchen at a posh resort outside of town. This was a great jumping-off point for developing and applying my personal culinary style. Jeanne, my wife, who has the personality and know-how, ran the dining room in a fun but food-serious way. People loved the experience, and we acquired quite a large group of loyal "foodies." We were there for over a year, but we really wanted to move into town with the Santa Fe dining scene. That's when, to my good fortune, some mutual friends introduced me to Cliff Skoglund.

During the interview, Cliff was ardent; he spoke of his early days as a chef, before he was a successful businessman, restaurateur, furniture designer, and owner of a nightclub and contemporary art gallery. He aspired to create a truly unique and world-class restaurant. He wanted to produce the best food he and a chef possibly could, and he wanted to place someone in the kitchen with the same vim and vigor that he had displayed throughout his career.

Listening to the clarity and passion of his dedication was inspiring. He spoke of his vision for Geronimo's future. It was enthralling and made me want to hear a lot more. What really sold me, though, was the way he talked about food: where he liked to eat, and what he genuinely loved about food. He really knew what he was talking about. Besides having a beautiful restaurant and an unrivaled zeal for hospitality and excellence, he loved food. My thoughts were simple: Sign me up!

That was quite a few years ago, and to this day the work I do here at Geronimo, is fueled not only by my own fervor

for originality and excellence, but also by Cliff's enthusiasm and wisdom. I value his friendship and have tremendous respect for him and what he has accomplished.

Eric on . . . Memory Lane; Cliff Notes

Tequila Lime Tarts

This recipe comes from my pastry apprenticeship with Russell Dingeldein, an ultra-talented pastry chef, a generous teacher, and a wonderful human being. He was a tough cookie—nothing got by him. If a chocolate cream pie had too much or too little filling, well, you'd better come in the next day with your toque hung low. This is Russell's Key lime pie, with a little tequila added, for a New Mexican flair. It's one of our most popular desserts and is quite refreshing. For this recipe, you will need four 3 by 3 inches in diameter and 2 inches tall metal ring molds or tart rings, and the tarts need to cool for 8 hours before serving.

CRUST

2 tablespoons unsalted butter, melted

3/4 cup graham cracker crumbs

FILLING

2 eggs, separated

3/4 cup sweetened condensed milk

2 tablespoons freshly squeezed Key lime juice

1 tablespoon 100% Blue Agave tequila (we use El Tesoro Silver)

Whipped cream, for garnish

8 Key lime slices, for garnish

To prepare the crust, in a bowl, combine the graham cracker crumbs and butter, and mix thoroughly.

Preheat the oven to 300°F. Line a baking pan with parchment paper. Place the 4 ring molds, 3 inches across and 2 inches deep, on the parchment.

Measure 3 tablespoons of the crust mixture into each of the ring molds. Press and pack the crumbs to create a flat 1/2-inch-thick base.

Place in the oven and bake for 8 minutes, until the crust is set. Remove from the oven and set on a rack to cool.

To prepare the filling, in an electric mixer fitted with the whip attachment, whip together the egg yolks and condensed milk on medium-high speed until pale and doubled in volume. Set the mixer speed to low and slowly add the lime juice and tequila. Mix until incorporated. Using a rubber spatula, transfer to a large bowl.

Make sure the bowl and whip of the electric mixer are thoroughly clean; the egg whites can't whip properly if any grease is present in the bowl.

In an electric mixer fitted with the whip attachment, whip the egg whites on high speed until soft peaks form. Using the rubber spatula, slowly and carefully fold the egg whites, in 3 additions, into the lime mixture. Try not to over mix, as this will deflate the volume of the filling. Gently transfer this filling equally into the cooled shells.

Preheat the oven to 325°F.

Place the tarts in the oven and bake for 8 to 10 minutes, until just set and pale yellow in color. They are very fragile. Treat them as you would a soufflé, because they will fall if handled roughly.

Before unmolding the tarts, refrigerate them for at least 8 hours.

Chill 4 dessert plates.

Remove the tarts from the refrigerator. Dip a thin-bladed knife into boiling water, and wipe dry. Carefully run the knife between the tart shell and the inside of the ring mold. Gently lift the ring mold free of the tart. Using a large metal spatula, transfer each tart to a chilled dessert plate.

Serve with whipped cream and garnish with Key lime slices.

Cheese

Feta Cheese with Hot Minted Fingerling Potatoes

Serves 4

New Mexico's own Tucumcari Mountain Cheese Factory (see page 221) supplies feta cheese to Greek restaurants in such markets as Houston, Phoenix, Chicago, New York, Boston, and Los Angeles. In fact, after producing 3.75 million pounds of feta last year, Tucumcari Mountain ranks as the fifth or sixth largest producer of feta in the United States. That's a stunning statistic for a town with a small population, best known to Route 66 aficionados as the easternmost destination in New Mexico, and famous for its 200 motels! This fresh mint combined with the cheese and potatoes in this recipe makes reference to summery Greek salads. With a big red wine or a glass of ouza this would make an excellent appetizer, or late night supper.

MINTED FINGERLING POTATOES

8 ounces fingerling potatoes

1 tablespoon unsalted butter

1 shallot, sliced

2 slices applewood-smoked bacon, cooked and very finely diced

2 tablespoons capers

Kosher salt

Freshly ground black pepper

SALAD

1 cup mâche, washed and dried

$1/2$ cup fresh raspberries

$1/4$ teaspoon very finely diced red onion

2 tablespoons basic vinaigrette (page 203)

4 slices feta cheese, $1/2$ inch thick (about 4 ounces)

Place the potatoes in a pot of salted water to cover. Place over medium-high heat and bring to a boil. Cook until tender when pierced with a fork. Remove from the heat. Transfer to a colander and drain. Allow to cool to room temperature. Transfer to a cutting surface and slice into $1/4$-inch-thick circles.

Place a sauté pan over medium heat and add the butter. When the butter starts to bubble and turn brown, add the shallot and cook for 1 minute, until translucent. Add the potatoes, bacon, capers, and salt and pepper to taste and sauté for 2 minutes, until heated thoroughly. Remove from the heat.

To prepare the salad, place the mâche, raspberries, and onion in a small, chilled bowl. Sprinkle with the vinaigrette and gently toss to coat.

Set out 4 salad plates.

Lay a slice of the cheese on each plate, and spoon the potatoes equally over the cheese. Arrange little mounds of the mâche salad atop. Serve immediately.

Vermont Cheddar Tempura with Sautéed Caramel Fuji Apples

Serves 4

Tempura cheese! What was I thinking in today's health-conscious world? Everyone needs a treat now and then, however, and the wonderful taste of this aged cheddar, with its perfect sharpness, melting over sweet apples and toast is one to indulge in! I use Grafton Village's award-winning reserve Cheddar (see page 220). Their cheese is handcrafted and made with milk from Vermont Jersey cows, which is famous for its high butterfat content. Blessed are the cheesemakers!

For this recipe, you will need a loaf of sliced fresh brioche and a deep-fat fryer or frying thermometer.

12 ounces Vermont cheddar cheese

1 cup all-purpose flour

SAUTÉED APPLES

2 Fuji apples

2 tablespoons unsalted butter

2 tablespoons superfine sugar

Pinch of salt

1/8 teaspoon freshly ground cinnamon

Pinch of freshly ground white pepper

4 cups peanut oil, for deep-fat frying

TEMPURA BATTER

1 cup all-purpose flour

1 egg

1 egg yolk

1 cup ice-cold pilsner beer

2 tablespoons minced green onion

4 slices fresh brioche

Using a warm, sharp knife, slice the cheese into 4 equal rectangles. Place the cheese on a plate, and dust with 1/2 cup of the flour. Cover the cheese and place in the freezer for 1 hour.

To prepare the apples, peel, core, and halve the apples and slice the halves 1/4 inch thick. Place a sauté pan over medium heat and add the butter. When the butter is melted and brown, add the apples and sugar. Cook, stirring frequently, for about 5 minutes, until the sugar has caramelized on the apples. Add the salt, cinnamon, and pepper and stir just to blend. Remove from the heat.

Pour the oil into a deep-fat fryer and preheat to 350°F.

To prepare the tempura, place the flour in a bowl and create a well. Place the egg, egg yolk, beer, and green onion into the center of the flour, and whisk just until combined.

Prepare a plate with several layers of paper towels. Warm 4 dessert plates.

Remove the cheese from the freezer and dust with the remaining 1/2 cup flour. Carefully dip the cheese into the tempura batter. Make sure that each piece is thoroughly coated with the batter, and then gently lower the pieces, one at a time, into the fryer. Turn them once. Fry for about 2 minutes, until they are evenly colored a rich golden brown. Transfer to the paper towels to drain.

Toast the brioche slices in a toaster until golden brown. Trim the crust, and slice in half on the diagonal.

Arrange 2 brioche toast points on each plate, and evenly divide the sautéed apples onto the toast. Set a piece of cheese tempura atop the apples. Serve immediately.

Brie de Meaux with Anise Poached Kumquats, Grape Must, and Chervil Salad

Serves 4

Brie de Meaux is often called the mother of all soft—white or bloomy—rind cheeses. It is smooth, voluptuous, and not as runny as some Bries can be. The aroma is that of earthy mushrooms. Here we accompany it with some sweets: the thick, honeyed, almost chocolatey grape must (see page 221) and candied kumquats.

POACHED KUMQUATS

30 ripe kumquats

1 cup water

1 cup turbinado sugar

2 tablespoons anisette

4 star anise pods

CHERVIL SALAD

1 cup fresh chervil leaves

1/2 small red onion, julienned

2 tablespoons light olive oil

1 teaspoon apple cider vinegar

Pinch of kosher salt

12 ounces Brie de Meaux, at room temperature

8 round croutons, 2 inches across (page 206)

2 tablespoons grape must (see page 221)

To prepare the kumquats, wash the kumquats and remove any stems. Place a saucepan over medium heat and add the kumquats and the water. Bring to a boil and cook, stirring frequently, for 20 minutes, until the kumquats begin to soften. Add the sugar, anisette, and star anise, and stir. Decrease the heat to medium-low and cook for 20 minutes, until the liquid begins to thicken and the kumquats begin to wrinkle and collapse into themselves.

Cover and refrigerate overnight.

Remove the kumquats from the refrigerator and strain over a small bowl. Be sure to reserve the syrup and use it for a special dessert sauce; it's terrific over vanilla ice cream.

To prepare the salad, combine the chervil leaves, onions, olive oil, cider vinegar, and salt in a small bowl. Gently toss to coat.

Set out 4 salad plates.

Cut the Brie into 4 equal servings. Arrange a piece of cheese and a little ramekin of the kumquats on each plate. Set 2 croutons on each plate, and mound the salad atop them. Spoon a puddle of the grape must around the crouton. Serve immediately.

Stir with the handle end of a wooden spoon until all the liquids come together. Slowly work in the flour from the sides until the dough becomes difficult to stir.

Clean all the pasta off the spoon and begin working the mixture with your hands. Form a ball and knead for about 5 minutes, until smooth. If the dough sticks to the surface, add a bit more flour, a little at a time.

Wrap the dough tightly in plastic wrap. Refrigerate for at least 1 hour, to rest the dough.

Variation: For the Shrimp Ravioli (page 101), stir 1 tablespoon tomato paste into the dough when you add the eggs.

Simple Syrup

$1/2$ teaspoon lemon zest
2 cups sugar
1 cup water

Combine the lemon zest, sugar, and water in a saucepan. Place over medium heat and bring to a simmer. Cook for 5 minutes. Remove from the heat. Strain through a chinois into a bowl. Place over a larger bowl filled with ice water to lower the temperature quickly. Use immediately or transfer to an airtight storage container and refrigerate. This will keep for up to 2 weeks.

Sun-Dried Tomato Oil

4 cups water
1 cup sun-dried tomatoes

$1^1/2$ cups light olive oil
$1/4$ cup coarsely chopped yellow onion
1 teaspoon coarsely chopped garlic

Pour the water into a saucepan and bring to a boil over medium-high heat. Fill a bowl with ice water. Blanch the tomatoes in the boiling water for 2 minutes. Using a spider or slotted spoon, immediately transfer the tomatoes into the ice water bath. Shock for 2 minutes. Transfer to a colander and drain.

Place a saucepan over medium heat and add $1/2$ cup of the olive oil. When the oil is hot, add the onion and garlic. Cook for about 2 minutes, or until the onion is translucent and begins to brown slightly. Remove from the heat and add the tomatoes and the remaining 1 cup of oil. Transfer to a blender and purée until smooth. Strain through a fine chinois into a bowl. Press down with a rubber spatula to remove all the oil from the pulp. Use immediately or transfer to an airtight storage container and refrigerate. This will keep for up to 1 week.

Scraping Seeds from a Vanilla Bean

Using a small, sharp knife, split the vanilla bean in half lengthwise. Using the dull side of a narrow table knife, carefully scrape the pulpy seeds into a small bowl.

If you don't need the pods for your recipe, rinse them and dry thoroughly in a low (250°F) oven, and then place them in your bags of granulated and powdered sugar. They add delicious aroma and subtle flavor to the sugar.

Veal Demi-Glace

Determine how much demi-glace you need, and pour twice that amount of veal stock into a saucepan. Set over medium heat. Bring to a simmer. Decrease the heat to medium-low and simmer until the stock reduces to half its volume and is thick and syrupy. Use immediately or transfer to an airtight storage container and refrigerate. This will keep for up to 1 week.

White Butter Sauce (Beurre Blanc)

1 teaspoon unsalted butter
2 tablespoons minced shallot
1 sprig thyme
1 bay leaf
10 peppercorns
1 cup dry white wine
$1/2$ cup champagne vinegar
1 cup unsalted butter, cut into 1-inch cubes and refrigerated
Pinch of kosher salt

Place a small saucepan over medium-low heat and add the butter. When the butter has melted, add the shallot, thyme, bay leaf, and peppercorns. Sauté for about 1 minute, or until the shallot becomes translucent.

Pour in the white wine and champagne vinegar and decrease the heat to low. Simmer for about 5 minutes, until the liquid is reduced to about $1/4$ cup. Slowly add the chilled butter cubes, piece by piece, stirring constantly with a wooden spoon until all the butter is incorporated. Remove from the heat immediately and strain through a chinois into a bowl. Gently press out all of the sauce. Add the salt and set aside in a warm, but not hot, place.

Use immediately, as this sauce does not keep.

Little Critical Stocks

Blonde Chicken Stock

6 pounds chicken bones and feet
5 quarts water (filtered is best)
1 cup diced peeled carrots
2 cups diced yellow onion
1 cup diced leek
$1/_2$ cup diced celery
16 black peppercorns
1 bay leaf

Place the bones and feet in a colander and rinse under cold running water. Remove any organ meat, such as livers and hearts, which would cloud the stock. Transfer the bones to a large pot and cover with cold water. Place over high heat and bring to a simmer. Carefully pour the contents of the pot into a colander set in the sink and drain off all the liquid.

Rinse the bones again under cold running water. This step draws out impurities that would cloud the stock and possibly cause bitterness.

Rinse out the pot and return the bones to the pot. Fill with cold water to cover. Place over medium-high heat and bring to a simmer. Using a ladle, gently skim off the impurities that form on the surface. Decrease the heat to medium-low and keep the stock at a simmer. Continue simmering for 1 hour, until the amount of impurities starts to lessen.

Add the carrots, onions, leeks, celery, peppercorns, and bay leaf. Simmer slowly for 1 more hour. Be careful never to let the stock come to a rolling boil, because it will become cloudy.

Strain the liquid through a fine chinois into a bowl, and place it over a larger bowl filled with ice water to lower the temperature quickly. Transfer the finished stock to an airtight storage container and refrigerate or freeze. This will keep for 3 days refrigerated and for up to 1 month if frozen.

Brown Chicken Stock

6 pounds chicken bones and feet

1 tablespoon kosher salt

$^1/_4$ cup canola oil

2 tablespoons tomato paste

1 cup peeled diced carrots

2 cups diced yellow onion

5 quarts water (filtered is best)

1 cup diced leek

16 black peppercorns

1 bay leaf

Preheat the oven to 400°F.

Place the bones and feet in a colander and rinse under cold running water. Remove any organ meat, such as livers and hearts, which would cloud the stock. Transfer the bones to a baking pan, and sprinkle with the salt and drizzle with the oil.

Place in the oven and roast for 30 minutes, until the bones are golden brown. Remove from the oven and dollop the tomato paste over the bones. Arrange the carrots and onions over the top. Place the bones and vegetables (mirepoix) back in the oven for 15 more minutes, until they begin to caramelize. Remove from the oven and let cool.

Transfer the roasted bones and mirepoix to a large pot. Cover with water to at least 2 inches over the bones. Add the leeks, peppercorns, and bay leaf. Place the pot over medium-high heat and bring to a simmer. Decrease the heat to medium-low. Frequently skim off any foam and excess fat that rises to the surface. Simmer for $1^1/_2$ hours. Remove from the heat. Carefully strain through a fine chinois into a bowl. Place over a larger bowl filled with ice water to lower the temperature quickly.

Transfer the finished stock to an airtight storage container and refrigerate or freeze. This will keep for 1 week refrigerated and for up to 1 month if frozen.

Court-Bouillon

2 cups white wine

2 cups water

2 tablespoons white vinegar

Freshly squeezed juice of 1 lemon

1 bouquet garni (page 205)

1 yellow onion, diced

1 stalk celery

5 Italian parsley stems

10 black peppercorns

Combine all the ingredients in a large saucepan and place over medium heat. Decrease the heat to medium-low and simmer for 30 minutes, until the flavors meld. Remove from the heat. Strain through a fine chinois into a bowl. Use the court-bouillon immediately, or place it over a larger bowl filled with ice water to chill. Transfer to an airtight storage container and refrigerate. This will keep for up to 2 days.

Fish Stock

2 tablespoons light olive oil

4 pounds lean white fish bones, chopped with a cleaver (halibut, fluke, sea bass)

1 cup diced white onion

$1/4$ cup chopped shallot

$1/4$ cup coarsely chopped celery

4 cups dry white wine

1 bouquet garni (page 205)

1 cup mushroom trimmings (avoid trimmings with black gills)

Place a large stockpot over medium heat and add the olive oil. When the oil is hot, add the fish bones, onion, shallot, and celery and sauté for 5 minutes, until the vegetables begin to cook.

Deglaze the pan with the white wine. Add the bouquet garni and mushroom trimmings, and enough water to just cover. Decrease the heat to low and simmer for 30 minutes.

Strain through a fine chinois into a bowl. Set the bowl over a larger bowl filled with ice water and chill.

Transfer to an airtight storage container and refrigerate. This will keep for up to 2 days.

Lobster Stock

3 pounds uncooked lobster shells

$1/4$ cup light olive oil

2 leeks, washed and sliced

$1/2$ white onion, thinly sliced

$1/2$ cup peeled and thinly sliced carrots

1 cup chopped celery

2 tablespoons tomato paste

6 sprigs Italian parsley

1 cup chopped fresh fennel bulb

2 cups white wine

1 tablespoon crustacean spice (page 206)

8 cups blonde chicken stock (page 213)

Rinse and dry the lobster shells. If you're using the heads, remove and discard the gills and stomach. Wrap the shells in a large, sturdy towel and crush with the back of an old knife or a mallet.

Place a heavy-bottomed pot over medium-high heat, and add the oil. When the oil is hot, add the shells and cook for about 10 minutes, until bright red. Add the leeks, onion, carrots, and celery. Decrease the heat to medium and cook for 15 minutes, until the vegetables are softened but not browned. Stir in the tomato paste and cook for 2 minutes. Add the parsley, chopped fennel, wine, crustacean spice, and chicken stock. Bring back to a simmer, and cook gently for 1 to $1^1/2$ hours, until the flavors meld.

Strain the stock through a chinois into a bowl. Place over a larger bowl filled with ice water to lower the temperature quickly. Use immediately or transfer to an airtight storage container and refrigerate or freeze. This will keep for up to 3 days in the refrigerator and for up to a month in the freezer.

Shrimp Stock

1/4 cup light olive oil

3 pounds uncooked shrimp shells, rinsed and dried

2 leeks, sliced

1/2 white onion, thinly sliced

1/2 cup peeled and thinly sliced carrots

1 cup chopped celery

2 tablespoons tomato paste

6 sprigs Italian parsley

2 cups white wine

1 tablespoon crustacean spice (page 206)

8 cups blonde chicken stock (page 213)

Place a heavy-bottomed pot over medium-high heat and add the oil. When the oil is hot, add the shells and cook for about 10 minutes, until bright red. Add the leeks, onion, carrots, and celery. Decrease the heat to medium, and cook for 15 minutes, until the vegetables are softened but not browned. Stir in the tomato paste and cook for 2 minutes. Add the parsley, wine, crustacean spice, and chicken stock. Bring back up to a simmer, and cook gently for 1 hour, until the flavors meld. Strain the stock through a chinois into a bowl. Place the bowl in a larger bowl filled with ice water to lower the temperature quickly. Use immediately or transfer to an airtight storage container and refrigerate or freeze. This will keep for up to 3 days in the refrigerator and up to a month in the freezer.

Veal Stock

Water

2 tablespoons salt

Dash of vinegar

10 pounds veal bones, cut into 2-inch pieces (if possible, use a mixture of marrow bones [femur] and neck bones)

3 cups coarsely diced yellow onion

1 cup peeled, coarsely diced carrot

1 cup coarsely diced celery

1 cup diced leek

4 cloves garlic, split

2 cups diced ripe tomato

2 tablespoons tomato paste

1 bouquet garni (page 205)

10 black peppercorns

2 bay leaves

Fill a large pot with water and bring to a boil over high heat. Add the salt and vinegar, and bring to a boil. Add the bones. Cook and stir for 1 minute. Drain the bones into a colander. Rinse well under cold running water to remove any impurities.

Preheat the oven to 450°F.

Arrange the bones in a large roasting pan and place in the oven. Roast for 45 minutes, until dark brown and the marrow begins to seep out.

Decrease the temperature to 400°F and cook for another 45 minutes, until the bones are dark and rich in color.

Remove the pan from the oven and place the bones in a large stockpot.

The roasting pan will have crusty meat drippings sticking to the bottom. Scrape these off with a wooden spoon and put them in the pot with the bones.

In the same roasting pan, place the onion, carrot, celery, leek, garlic, tomatoes, and tomato paste and stir together. Place the vegetables in the oven and roast for 20 minutes, until brown.

Transfer the vegetables (mirepoix) to the pot with the bones, scraping the bottom of the pan to get any remnants. Add the bouquet garni, black peppercorns, and bay leaves to the pot. Cover with water, at least 2 inches over the bones. Place over medium-high heat and bring to a quiet boil. Decrease the heat to medium-low, and keep the stock at a low simmer. Using a ladle, gently skim off the impurities that form on the surface, without stirring the stock.

Simmer the stock for 6 hours, adding more water as needed to keep the bones covered. Remove from the heat. Strain the stock through a large-holed chinois into a large bowl, letting all the liquid drain off the bones. Strain through a fine chinois into a large bowl, to remove all the particles.

Place over a larger bowl filled with ice water and chill. Use immediately or transfer to an airtight storage container and refrigerate or freeze. This will keep for up to 1 week in the refrigerator and for up to 1 month in the freezer.

Little Critical Techniques

Blanching and Shocking

To blanch means to cook quickly in boiling salted water. Usually the blanched item is then plunged immediately into an ice water bath to "shock" and halt the cooking process.

The best way to blanch successfully is to use a lot more water than you think you will need, both for boiling the vegetables and for the ice water bath.

Blanching preserves color and flavor when the ratio of water to salt is accurate. Bring the water to a rolling boil and add a generous amount of salt to the water: about $1/4$ cup of salt for every quart of water.

Before you begin, wash, trim, and prepare all the vegetables that you are going to blanch, and prepare a large bowl of ice water.

Vegetables vary widely in the amount of time they require for blanching. For example, it takes only 15 seconds to blanch basil and other fragile herbs. Blanching extra-large asparagus may take as long as 10 minutes.

The important thing with blanching is that the water return to a rolling boil as soon as possible after the item is added. This usually requires blanching vegetables in small batches.

Testing the vegetables as you go is important. Using a slotted spoon, lift a piece out during the cooking process and test its doneness with a knife. The goal is for the vegetable to be cooked through, yet still crisp. Eventually, as you develop a feel for the process of blanching, you will recognize the change in appearance that indicates doneness.

Frenching

To french a rack of lamb, using a boning knife, trim the cartilage off the saddle end. Flip the rack over and make a slit into meat along the ends of bones (2 to 4 inches, depending on length of bones). Trim the fat and meat from the ends of the bones. Carve the meat from between each of the rib bones. Continue trimming the meat off all the bones in the rack. Scrape the bones clean with a knife or a piece of clean steel wool.

Pork chops, chicken wings, pheasant breasts, may be frenched by trimming the meat away from the bone, leaving the bone clean and exposed.

Peeling Tomatoes

1 gallon water

2 tablespoons salt

2 pounds tomatoes

Fill a large pot with the water and add the salt. Place over high heat, and bring to a rolling boil. Fill a large bowl with 1 gallon of ice water.

Cut out the stem ends of the tomatoes. Using a very sharp knife, lightly score a small "x" into the skin on the other end. Plunge the tomatoes into the boiling water for 1 to 2 minutes, until the skin begins to peel back.

Using a spider or slotted spoon, remove the tomatoes and transfer into the ice water bath.

Shock for about 1 minute, or until thoroughly chilled. When cool, use a small paring knife to peel back a corner of the skin where it has been scored; the rest of the skin will come away easily.

Toasting Coconut

Preheat the oven to 400°F.

Spread the shredded coconut on a baking pan. Toast in the oven for 8 to 10 minutes, until the ends of the coconut turn golden brown. Allow to cool for a few minutes.

Toasting Nuts

Preheat the oven to 400°F.

Oil a sheet tray, and spread out the nuts. Toast in the oven for 10 to 15 minutes, until they turn golden brown. Allow to cool for a few minutes.

Toasting Seeds

Place a dry pan over medium-high heat and add the seeds. Shake the pan continuously until the seeds are lightly browned and remove from the pan immediately. Cool before using.

Tournéed Vegetables

Peel the vegetable, and cut large round or oval vegetables, such as beets and potatoes, into quarters, sixths and eighths, to form pieces slightly larger than 2 inches. Cut cylindrical vegetables, such as carrots, into 2 inch pieces.

Using a sharp paring knife, carve the pieces into barrel or football shapes, with either 5 or 7 smooth, evenly spaced faces, tapered so that both ends are narrower than the center.

Sources and Resources

Bacon Nueske's, of Wittenberg, Wisconsin, produces some of the finest bacon you'll ever eat. It's very lean and is slowly smoked over local applewood, giving it a distinctive, rich, smoky flavor and aroma. Their hams are wonderful as well.

> Contact them at:
> www.nueske.com
> (800) 392-2266

Balsamic vinegar Fondo di Trebbiano produces a true balsamic vinegar of Modena, barrel aged for 25 years. It is prepared according to ancient traditions: Trebbiano grape must is blended with strong red wine vinegar and then moved through a succession of hardwood casks, resulting in a brilliant, dark brown vinegar.

> Contact them at:
> www.cybercucina.com
> (800) 796-0116

Carnaroli rice This rice is acknowledged to be some of the very finest available for creamy risotto dishes. Alimentitalia is a good source for this product.

> Contact them at:
> www.italianfoods.com
> (510) 595-3832

Cheddar cheese Grafton Village Cheese Company in Grafton, Vermont, makes a Super Aged Cheddar, 30 to 36 months old, with an extra creamy, robust flavor.

> Contact them at:
> www.graftonvillagecheese.com
> (800) 472-3866

Chicken Pollo Real/Real Chicken, located in Socorro, New Mexico, is the largest certified organic, pastured poultry operation in the United States. Pollo Real chickens are grass-fed. The birds are moved daily onto fresh, organically certified grasses with fresh air and sunshine. They eat organic grains and are processed in organically certified facilities. The chickens are available year round as whole fryers, whole roasters, and cut-up fryers. Shipping is by UPS or priority mail.

> Contact them at:
> http://organicchicken.com
> (505) 838-0345

Feta cheese Chuck Krause, a fourth-generation cheesemaker from Wisconsin, started the Tucumcari Mountain Cheese Factory in 1996. His efforts to market cheddar couldn't compete with larger producers, but a Houston-based Greek food wholesaler convinced him to try making feta cheese. An order that began with 2 pallets has now grown to 700 pallets a year, and Chuck's feta products are trucked all over the country. The cheese is made from fresh, local milk from dairies run, in most cases, by third- and fourth-generation farmers. Krause takes pleasure in making cheese "the old way," and his wife sells the feta and their hand-crafted kalamata feta and tomato-basil and green chile jack cheese at her shop.

    Contact them at:
    Mediterranean Café and Cheese Store
    (505) 461-3755

Foie gras Hudson Valley produces a velvety, meaty foie made solely of duck liver. This is a luxurious, delectable product that holds up well to searing.

    Contact them at:
    www.hudsonvalleyfoiegras.com
    (845) 292-2500

Grape must Sapori d'Emilia produces a high-quality grape must.

    Contact them at:
    www.saporidemilia.it

Iroquois cornmeal A Santa Fe-based organization, the Collective Heritage Institute has succeeded in reviving an ancient, heirloom maize, Iroquois corn. Historically and ecologically significant, as well as delicious, this corn has never hybridized and has been in continuous cultivation by the Iroquois people for centuries. The corn, once in danger of becoming extinct, is now being cultivated, harvested, roasted, and distributed, through the tenacious efforts of native Iroquois growers. It is available as flour, whole hominy (posole), and tamal flour.

    Contact them at:
    www.bioneers.org
    (888) 652-5628

Kitchen tools Las Cosas Kitchen Shoppe & Cooking School, located in Santa Fe, is a kindred spirit in their attitudes about cooking: they are in it for the fun and the beauty! This is the place for all sorts of cooking equipment.

    Las Cosas is also a good source for many of the gourmet and specialty foods called for in the recipes.

    Contact them at:
    www.lascosascooking.com
    (877) 299-7184

New Mexico green chile Bueno Foods is one of the Southwest's premier producers of New Mexican and Mexican cuisine, still owned and operated by a long-time New Mexican family. The company offers and ships more than 150 authentic New Mexican and Mexican food products, including flame roasted fresh frozen green chile, red chile, salsas and sauces, tortillas, dried chile pods and chile powders, tamales, enchiladas and more.

    Contact them at:
    www.buenofoods.com
    (800) 952-4453

Smithfield ham Genuine Smithfield hams are dry salt-cured and then spiced and slowly smoked using oak, hickory, and applewood. Aged for nearly a year, then cooked and closely trimmed, these hams have terrific flavor.

Contact them at:

www.smithfieldcollection.com

(800) 628-2242

Smoked pork loin Groff Meats Inc., a small, family-owned and family-operated shop in Elizabethtown, Pennsylvania, specializes in fresh and smoked meats. The business has been in the family for four generations. Their smoked pork loin is out of this world, and they ship their smoked meats, sausages, bacon, and hams, all over the United States.

Contact them at:

(717) 367-1246

Tahitian vanilla beans Tahitian vanilla is truly a splendid spice. NUI Enterprises imports high-quality vanilla beans, expertly cured to perfect moisture content on the island of Raiatea. They also sell Tahitian vanilla extract. Orders can be placed online.

Contact them at:

http://store.yahoo.com/vanillafromtahiti/localmerchants.html

Verjus Napa Valley Verjus produces an ultra-high-quality verjus, both red and white.

Contact them at:

www.lentia.com

Wasabi Pacific Farm Wasabi grows, harvests, and ships its fresh wasabi products by air to Japan and throughout the United States. They are located near the central Pacific coast of Oregon and are the only commercial North American grower of this rare and difficult-to-grow vegetable.

Contact them at:

www.freshwasabi.com

(800) 927-2248

Glossary of Unusual Ingredients and Cooking Terms

Amuse-Gueule (ah-mewz GEURL): Chef's tasting; a one or two-bite portion of something exotic, unusual or otherwise special that is served before the first course, to tickle the appetite.

Batonnets (bat-tah-NAYS): Foods cut into small stick (baton) shapes.

Bouchée (boo-SHAY): The French word for "mouthful," a bouchée is a bite-size puff pastry shell that can be filled with savory or sweet fillings.

Bouquet garni (boo-KAY gahr-NEE): A bunch of herbs, classically a trio of parsley, thyme, and bay leaf, that are tied together or placed in a cheesecloth bag and used to flavor broths, soups, or stews.

Brunoise (broo-NWAHZ): A method of dicing very, very finely. The term is usually, but not exclusively, used to refer to the preparation of staple root vegetables, such as carrots, onions, turnips, and leeks.

Caper: The flower bud of a shrub native to eastern Asia and parts of the Mediterranean. The small buds are used as a condiment, either pickled in vinegar or preserved in brine, and add a pungent, piquant flavor to a variety of sauces and dishes. The petite nonpareil caper from southern France is considered the finest.

Capsicum (KAP-sih-kuhm): Any of hundreds of varieties of fruit-bearing plants called peppers, all of which are in the nightshade family.

Carnaroli rice (car-na-ROW-lee): A super-fino grade of short, plump-grained Italian rice from Novara and Vercelli. The high starch content of this rice gives risotto its characteristic creaminess.

Chiffonade (shihf-uh-NAHD): French for "made of rags," these are thin strips or shreds of vegetables, traditionally sorrel and lettuce, either sautéed or used raw as garnish in soups.

Chile peppers: The fruit of the genus *Capsicum*, the pepper plant. There are 150 to 200 varieties of this plant, grown all around the world and spread by trade and cultivation, some measuring up to thousands on the Scoville scale of heat (the agreed-upon method of evaluating the gustatory heat of peppers).

Chine: The backbone of an animal, usually removed from the rib bones, in cuts such as a rack of lamb.

Chinois (sheen-WAH): A French sieve made of extremely fine metal mesh, cone shaped, with a rounded or slightly flattened bottom, used for straining. After the liquid has passed through, a heavy metal spoon or pestle is used to firmly compress the food solids, resulting in a very refined liquid essence.

Cipollini (chihp-oh-LEE-nee): The sweet little bulbs of the grape hyacinth, which look and taste like small onions and are sometimes called wild onions. They are served either raw or cooked.

Confit (kohn-FEE): An ancient method of preserving meat, usually goose (*confit d'oie*) or duck (*confit de canard*), described by Craig Claiborne as "one of the fabled glories of the French table." Our confit is prepared by rubbing legs of goose or duck with a mixture of thyme, rosemary, and sage, refrigerating overnight, and then cooking them in a simmering bath of duck fat until delectably tender. Confit may be stored in its own fat for up to 3 months.

Coulis (koo-LEE): A general term referring to a thick purée that may be used as a sauce or garnish.

Couverture: A professional-quality coating chocolate, with a 32 percent cocoa butter content that allows it to form a thin, extremely glossy shell.

Deglaze (dee-GLAYZ): Deglazing is done after food, usually meat, has been sautéed and removed from the pan. The excess fat is skimmed off, and a liquid, usually wine or stock, is heated in the pan and stirred to loosen the browned bits of food, creating a well-flavored mixture that can become a base for a sauce or gravy for the food that was just prepared.

Émincée (ahm-in-SAY): A meat or vegetable, that is very thinly sliced.

Entremettier (On-tra-met-teeah): The vegetable chef, or station, responsible for vegetables, starches, and pastas and sometimes soups.

Escalope (eh-skah-LAWP): The French term for a slice of meat or fish that has been pounded very thin. This tender cut requires only quick sautéing on both sides.

Flambé (flahm-BAY): French for "flamed" or "flaming," a technique that involves sprinkling food with liquor, which is then ignited to burn the alcohol off.

Fleur de sel (flurr-du-sell): The finest grade of pure, slightly sweet white sea salt, harvested along the coasts of France. Fleur de sel is produced only under certain specific weather conditions that cause these special mineral-rich crystals to rise to the water's surface, where they are culled by the paludier's "salt rakers."

French knife: Also called a chef's knife, this knife has a broad, tapered shape and a fine edge.

Frenched bones: Meat and poultry bones that have been prepared for cooking by having the meat scraped off.

Frisée (free-ZAY): A feathery, curly-leafed green in the chicory family, with a mildly bitter flavor.

Gari (GAH-ree): Also called *beni shoga*, this is ginger root that has been pickled in sweet vinegar and thinly sliced. It is used as a garnish, especially in Japanese dishes. Gari is also eaten to refresh the palate.

Glace de viande (glahs duh vee-AHND): A heavily reduced veal or beef stock of an almost syrupy, molasses-like consistency, used to rub meats as a finishing sauce.

Grape must: A rich, dark, sweet syrup made from freshly pressed, nonfermented juice of fully ripe grapes, often including pulp, skin, and seeds, and well strained before use. Grape must is excellent with buttery cheese, such as Bûcheron, and with foie gras.

Griswold: A shallow, wide, straight-sided pan, made of cast iron, that may have a single short handle, rather than the usual loop handles.

Hoisin (HOY-sihn): Also called Peking sauce, this thick, sweet-spicy sauce is widely used in Chinese cuisine as a table condiment and a flavoring for meat, poultry, and fish dishes. A mix of soybeans, garlic, chile peppers, and various spices, hoisin sauce appears in our elk marinade.

Jasmine rice: An aromatic rice from Thailand, with a distinctive fragrance and flavor.

Julienne (joo-lee-EHN): Food that has been cut into thin, matchstick strips, often used as a garnish.

Larding: To insert long, thin strips of fat, usually pork or bacon, into a dry cut of meat, in order to make the cooked meat more succulent, tender, and flavorful. These strips of fat are called lardons.

Lolla Rossa: A mild, tender, leaf lettuce with ruffled red edges.

Mâche: Also known as lamb's leaf or corn salad, this delicate green, native to Europe, grows as a rosette. The narrow, dark green leaves are exceptionally tender, with a tangy, nutlike flavor. It may also be cooked and served like spinach.

Mandoline (MAHN-duh-lihn): A compact, hand-operated machine with various adjustable blades that creates perfectly uniform paper-thin to thick slices, also useful for cutting foods into julienne.

Mirepoix (mihr-PWAH): A mixture of rather largely diced carrots, celery, and herbs sautéed in butter, used to season sauces, soups, or stews and as a bed on which to braise meats or fish.

Mise en place (MEEZ ahn plahs): A French term referring to having all the ingredients necessary for cooking a dish prepped and ready to combine.

Mizuna (mih-ZOO-nuh): A crisp, feathery green from Japan, frequently included in mesclun, a mix of specialty salad greens.

Nappé (nah-PAY): To coat food with a thin, even layer of sauce so that it is completely and lightly covered.

Noisette (nwah-ZEHT): French for "hazelnut," this term has come to mean a small, tender, round slice of lamb, beef, or veal, taken from the rib or loin.

Orach (OR-rick): A salad green with fleshy, triangular leaves and a slightly sweet flavor.

Panko (PAHN-koh): A coarse bread crumb used in Japanese cooking for coating fried foods. It creates a delicious, extra-crunchy crust.

Pâte sucrée (paht soo-KRAY): A butter-rich, sweetened pastry used for pie and tart crusts and filled cookies.

Pico de gallo (PEE-koh day GI-yoh): Spanish for "rooster's beak," pico de gallo is a picante salsa of finely chopped fresh onions, jalapeños, and tomatoes; fresh lime juice; salt; and various seasonings, such as garlic.

Pink salt: Also known as saltpeter and curing salt, pink salt acts as a preservative and is used in some chilled foie gras recipes to help the liver maintain a desirable pinkish color.

Poire-Williams (pwahr WEEL-yahms): A highly potent, crystal clear, pear-flavored distilled spirit, made in Switzerland and France.

Purée (pyuh-RAY): n. Any food that is finely mashed, processed, or blended to a smooth, thick consistency. v. To grind, process, blend, or force food through a sieve until it's completely smooth.

Quenelle (kuh-NEHL): A light, delicate dumpling made of seasoned, minced, or ground fish, meat, or vegetables, bound with eggs or panada (a thick paste made by mixing bread crumbs, flour, or rice with various liquids or egg yolks). The mixture is formed into small ovals and gently poached in stock.

Ramp: A bright green wild onion that grows all over North America, resembling a scallion with broad, thick leaves. With a powerful garlicky-onion flavor and aroma, the ramp may be used as a slightly stronger substitute for an onion, leek, or scallion.

Red orach: A purplish-red leafy salad green.

Reduce: To boil a liquid (usually stock, wine, or a sauce mixture) rapidly until the volume is reduced by evaporation, thickening the consistency and intensifying the flavor. The result is called a reduction.

Rondeau (RON-doe): A large, wide, straight-sided, heavy-bottomed pot, usually with loop handles.

Rösti, potatoes (RAW-stee, ROOSH-tee): Rösti, in Switzerland, means "crisp and golden." These are pancakes made of shredded potatoes, sautéed on both sides until crisp and browned.

Roulade (roo-LAHD): A slice of meat or fish rolled around a filling. Also, a rolled and filled sponge cake.

Sachet: A small bag or packet containing herbs or spices, used to season or flavor a soup, stew, or broth and removed at the end of the cooking period.

Sambal: A multipurpose spicy condiment, popular in Indonesia, Malaysia, and southern India. The most common form is sambal oelek, a mixture of chiles, brown sugar, and salt.

Sautoir (saw-TWARE): A shallow skillet with straight sides and a single, long handle, usually used for sautéing.

Sec: Dry, as a wine or Champagne, or used to describe a reduction in which all the liquid is cooked away.

Semifreddo (say-mee-FRAYD-doh): Italian for "half cold," this term refers to a variety of chilled or partially frozen desserts that may include, cake, custard, mousse, or whipped cream.

Shiso (SHEE-soh): An aromatic, jagged-edge leaf of the perilla plant, part of the basil and mint family. Used in salads and with sushi, it is also called perilla, or Japanese, basil and is available in Asian markets.

Shock: The method of plunging a cooked food into ice cold water to halt the cooking process immediately.

Spider: A long-handled coarse-mesh strainer, also called a skimmer.

Sweat: A method of cooking vegetables slowly in a small amount of fat over low heat in a very tightly covered pot. With this technique, the ingredients soften without browning and cook in their own juices.

Tamis (TAM-ee): Often called tammycloth or a drum sieve, a tamis is a large, round, flat-bottomed strainer, of cloth or fine mesh, used to strain liquid mixtures.

Tournéed (toor-NAYD): Foods, usually vegetables, that have been cut into barrel, olive, or football shapes.

Verjus (vehr-ZHOO): Literally "green juice," this is a tart, unfermented juice of unripe wine grapes, an indigenous product of the world's wine-growing regions. Verjus is used to add acidity to foods, like vinegar or lemon juice, but its more gentle acids are more wine compatible.

Zest: The perfumy outermost skin layer of citrus fruit, usually oranges and lemons.

There's a moment of satisfaction in the evening, a little peak of pleasure I get when I look across the dining room and see that the air is thick, that all kinds of conversations are happening, and I hear that wonderful hum. Every room is full, the bar is full, and there's that sound of all the action: people working, people eating, people having a really good time, enjoying fine wines. There's a fabulous sense of well-being. And to walk through it, through the different dining rooms and into the kitchen and back through: it's thrilling. There's a special excitement, almost a thickness in the air.

You could take a snapshot of it, and it would be the perfect setting in a restaurant.

It's an epiphany, a gorgeous moment, like when you've taken the first bite of something so delicious, so exactly what you were hoping for, and you go "aaaaah."

It's the flavor of the room, and in that moment all honor goes to everyone involved, especially the customers, because they have allowed us to do the thing we enjoy, which is to provide the Geronimo Experience, in just exactly this way: playful, beautiful, rich, enveloping.

The restaurant is alive, it's as if Geronimo has a heartbeat. You can hear it breathing. We're like athletes running at their best—heart beating at the right pace, breath in sync, running in a magnificent field. From the cooks to the chef to the host to the waiters, everyone is in the Zone. It's really extraordinary to watch.

The Geronimo Experience is all of this, and more: it's service, ambiance, food, it's the whole cast of characters, and it's a fabulous show. There's no detail too small. That's true at Geronimo every single night and every single lunch. There's no detail too small, from the beautiful service, the silver, the napkins, the texture of the bread basket, the herbs in the bread, *everything*.

Because this is what we do. And we have chosen to do it the absolute best that we can so that our best is always becoming better.

Cliff on . . . When Everything's Right

Index